Samarpan

With kind regards, ॐ and prem

Swami Niranjan

Samarpan

Living the Divine Connection

From the teachings of Swami Sivananda Saraswati
and Swami Satyananda Saraswati

Yoga Publications Trust, Munger, Bihar, India

© Sivananda Math 2008

All rights reserved. No part of this publication may be reproduced, transmitted or stored in a retrieval system, in any form or by any means, without permission in writing from Yoga Publications Trust.

The terms Satyananda Yoga® and Bihar Yoga® are registered trademarks owned by International Yoga Fellowship Movement (IYFM). The use of the same in this book is with permission and should not in any way be taken as affecting the validity of the marks.

Published by Yoga Publications Trust
First edition 2008

ISBN: 978-81-86336-69-4

Publisher and distributor: Yoga Publications Trust, Ganga Darshan, Munger, Bihar, India.

Website: www.biharyoga.net
www.rikhiapeeth.net

Printed at Thomson Press (India) Limited, New Delhi, 110001

Dedication

*In humility we offer this dedication to
Swami Sivananda Saraswati, who initiated
Swami Satyananda Saraswati into the secrets of yoga.*

Contents

Introduction   1

Samarpan
From the teachings of Swami Sivananda Saraswati
   1. Path of Samarpan   7
   2. Supreme Surrender   17
   3. Cultivation of Surrender   29
   4. Preparation and Qualifications   41
   5. The Four Jewels   50
   6. Transcendence of Desire   62
   7. Faith, Grace and Divine Will   76
   8. Guru-Disciple Relationship   85

Samarpan
From the teachings of Swami Satyananda Saraswati
   9. Origin of Samarpan   101
   10. Culmination of All Sadhana   105
   11. An Evolutionary Process   109
   12. Awakening Positive Forces   118
   13. Stepping into Samarpan   128
   14. Power of Faith   142
   15. Follow the Higher Will   152
   16. Role of the Guru   163
   17. Descent of Grace   175
   18. Living Samarpan   182
   19. Divine Communion   195

Glossary   207

Guru Pādukā Stotram

1. Anantasaṃsārasamudratāra-
   Naukāyitābhyāṃ gurubhaktidābhyām.
   Vairāgyasāmrājyadapūjanābhyām
   Namo namaḥ śrīgurupādukābhyām.

2. Kavitvavārāśiniśākarābhyām
   Daurbhāgyadāvāmbudamālikābhyām.
   Dūrīkṛtānamravipattitābhyām
   Namo namaḥ śrīgurupādukābhyām.

3. Natā yayoḥ śrīpatitāṃ samīyuḥ
   Kadāchidapyāśu daridravaryāḥ.
   Mūkāścha vāchaspatitāṃ hi tābhyām
   Namo namaḥ śrīgurupādukābhyām.

4. Nālikanīkāśapadāhṛtābhyām
   Nānāvimohādi nivārikābhyām.
   Namajjanābhīṣṭatatipradābhyām
   Namo namaḥ śrīgurupādukābhyām.

5. Nṛpālimaulivrajaratnakānti-
   Saridvirājajjhaṣakanyakābhyām.
   Nṛpatvadābhyāṃ natalokapaṅkteḥ
   Namo namaḥ śrīgurupādukābhyām.

6. Pāpāndhakārārka paramparābhyām
   Tāpatrayāhīndrakhageśvarābhyām.
   Jāḍyābdhisaṃśoṣaṇavāḍavābhyām
   Namo namaḥ śrīgurupādukābhyām.

7. Śamādiṣaṭkapradavaibhavābhyām
   Samādhidānavratadīkṣitābhyām.
   Ramādhavāṅghristhirabhaktidābhyām
   Namo namaḥ śrīgurupādukābhyām.

8. Svārchāparāṇāmakhileṣṭadābhyām
   Svāhāsahāyākṣadhurandharābhyām.
   Svāntāchchhabhāvaprada pūjanābhyām
   Namo namaḥ śrīgurupādukābhyām.

9. Kāmādisarpavrajagāruḍābhyām
   Vivekavairāgyanidhipradābhyām.
   Bodhapradābhyāṃ drutamokṣadābhyām
   Namo namaḥ śrīgurupādukābhyām.

Introduction

Samarpan is total offering to God of one's entire individual existence. It is a state in which the limited identity that separates the individual soul from the Divine, from the eternal oneness behind all forms, is transcended forever. This book presents the teachings on samarpan as expounded by two great spiritual masters, Swami Sivananda and Swami Satyananda. The concept of samarpan is taken beyond the usual descriptions of devotion and bhakti and revealed as the culmination of all spiritual sadhanas, through which an aspirant is able to transform himself into an instrument of the Divine, for the well-being of the entire creation.

Samarpan is the highest virtue and highest state of consciousness any spiritual aspirant can aspire for, when one is able to identify completely with the pure inner nature, the all-pervading, universal consciousness. It is an experience that dawns as a timeless moment when one's soul awakens to the reality that everything is a manifestation of the Divine. Every pleasure and sorrow is His, every breath is His miracle, and every day is His glory. Awakening to this moment, one begins to view and live life from a divine perspective, knowing beyond doubt that the entire manifest and unmanifest creation is but a play of the divine will; that life itself is nothing but His grace, and that we are simply instruments in His hands.

In the state of samarpan, when one is able to spontaneously surrender to the will of the Divine, life is permeated with bliss and becomes an uninterrupted flow of mystic communion and worship. It is only then, when communion with the Divine has been established, that the ultimate offering of the self can be made. The highest attainments of divine life are then offered for the welfare and spiritual upliftment of humanity.

These teachings, which reveal the magnitude and eternal splendour of samarpan, have a transformative quality which allows the reader a chance to be lifted out of ordinary everyday consciousness, way beyond the veil of limited individuality, into the transcendental persona of those who live upon this earth merged fully and completely in God. They introduce the reader to the highest mystical concepts of supreme love, devotion and humility; the power of faith and trust in oneself and God; perfect detachment and dispassion; supreme contentment and equanimity. The essence and necessity of the guru-disciple relationship is revealed, and the relevance of divine grace and divine will explained. The euphoric beauty of unconditional and absolute surrender to the Divine is held up before the reader as the final point of human evolution.

Thousands of spiritual aspirants have asked both Swami Sivananda and Swami Satyananda about self-surrender; how to practise it, and how to see and commune with God. The wisdom they have offered is presented here, as the eternal truths of the ancient science of yoga. The subtle realities of treading the path unfold, making it clear that mere intellectual study or verbal surrender is not enough to attain the goal. Self-surrender is not just thinking that one wants to surrender. Simply saying that one will leave everything in God's hands is not at all difficult. However, the application of samarpan in one's daily life is an entirely different matter, because through ignorance God has been forgotten. We have surrendered to the senses, to worldly enjoyments, and we are afraid of losing ourselves.

The whole process of samarpan unfolds over thousands of lifetimes as the individual searches for something that will give life a meaningful purpose. It is a process of awakening to the eternal essence within each and every human being, within everything that exists. It is process of becoming aware that we are trapped in a habitual, limited personality and seeing how one's identity is restricted to worldly roles, to infatuations with people, places and events. The very edifice of life is guided by one's self-centred ego: thoughts are guided by the ego, expectations are motivated by the ego, all efforts are energized by the ego, and all responses, reactions and identifications are associated with the ego. Consequently, a pertinent message of these teachings is that samarpan sadhana requires an irrevocable commitment, a single-minded devotion of head, heart and hand in order to transform the personal ego, step by step, into a selfless entity that lives for universal well-being. Only when empty of individual ego is one able to become God's instrument and live according to the divine will. Until then, it is not possible because the ego is the barrier between the human being and God.

Both Swami Sivananda and Swami Satyananda speak from their own enlightened understanding of the secrets of spiritual life. Their inspiration and guidance come from their own experiences of self-surrender; from their years of sincere and untiring service to guru and humanity; from their invaluable first hand encounters with the difficulties, sacrifices and frustrations that confront even the most dedicated spiritual aspirants; and from their own arduous austerities and sadhanas, which have taken them into profound states of cosmic consciousness, and allowed them to reach the heights of divine life.

If we can surrender ourself to God, the purpose of existence as a human being will have been achieved, for one who has realized God sees that God and His entire creation form a whole. Only one consciousness is seen everywhere. One consciousness has become the universe and everything in it.

In the words of Swami Satyananda: "When will you realize Him as the creator as well as the 'soul and stuff' of creation? He has expressed Himself in His creation; He is not separate from it. Just as ornaments made from gold are nothing but gold, and pots fashioned from clay are nothing but clay, His creation is nothing but His manifestation. Creation is nowhere without Him.

Everything is an expression of absolute consciousness. God is with form and without form; both are His attributes, they are one and the same. He reveals Himself in and through whatever form you choose to find Him. It is nothing but His grace, His will. Surrender the identity of your ego into God consciousness, because only then will He commune with you. Your individual consciousness must be totally consumed for this very purpose."

Samarpan

From the teachings of Swami Sivananda Saraswati

1
Path of Samarpan

Atma nivedana, complete surrendering of one's entire self to the Divine, is *samarpan*. In *Vishnu Sahasranama* it is said: "The heart of one who has taken refuge in and is wholly devoted to God is entirely purified, and he attains *Brahman*, the eternal." The devotee offers everything to God, including his body, mind and soul; he keeps nothing for himself. He loses even his own self in God. He becomes part and parcel of God and has no personal or independent existence. God takes care of the devotee who has surrendered completely to Him, and tests him as Himself.

The devotee treats happiness and sorrow, pleasure and pain, as gifts sent by God and is not attached to them. He does not feel egoistic, because he considers himself as an instrument in the hands of God. He has no ego, for his ego has gone over to God. He has no independent existence apart from God. God takes care of everyone and everything, including that which man cannot even dream of.

The devotee has no sensual craving, for his body is offered to God. He is not concerned with his body, for it is God's business to see to it. He only feels the presence of God and nothing else. He is fearless, for God is helping him at all times. He has no enemy, for he has given himself up to God, who has no enemies or friends. He has no anxiety, for by attaining the grace of God he has attained everything. He does not even have the thought of salvation; rather he does not want salvation. He merely wants God and nothing but God.

The devotee is satisfied with the love of God by which nothing is left unattained. What is there to be attained by one upon whom God has showered His grace? The devotee does not want to become sugar, but to taste sugar. There is pleasure in tasting sugar, but not in becoming sugar. So the devotee feels supreme joy in loving God, rather than in becoming God. God takes complete care of the devotee who says, "I am Thine," and who actually lives that.

Implications of self-surrender

> O Arjuna, surrender to Him with all your being. By His grace you will attain transcendental peace and the supreme, eternal abode.
>
> *(Bhagavad Gita, 18:62)*
>
> Abandon all duties and surrender to Me alone. I shall liberate you from all sins; fear not.
>
> *(Bhagavad Gita, 18:66)*

The gist of the teachings of Lord Krishna is found here. By living in the true spirit of these verses, the devotee realizes the goal of life soon; there is no doubt of this. Self-surrender must be pure, total, ungrudging and unreserved. Certain desires must not be kept for secret gratification. The real devotee will not ask the Lord for anything, not even for liberation. As long as the subtle desire for liberation lingers in the heart, one cannot claim to be a true devotee. Although the desire for emancipation is of a sattwic nature, the devotee is still a slave to it, so he remains selfish and unfit to call himself a sincere lover of God. He has not yet made total, unreserved self-surrender. To ask for liberation is a form of hypocrisy. How can a true devotee dare to ask anything of the Lord, when he knows that He is an ocean of love and compassion?

A real devotee never complains about God. The insincere devotee speaks ill of God when he is in distress. He says, "I have done twenty-five lakhs of japa and study the *Bhagavata* daily, yet God is not pleased with me. He has not removed my sufferings. God is deaf. He has not heard my prayers. What sort of God is He? Why should I have faith in Him?" But the real devotee rejoices in pain and suffering. He welcomes grief and sorrow, so that he may not forget God even for a second. He has the firm belief that God does everything for his good only. Kunti Devi prayed to Krishna: "O Lord, always give me pain, for only then will I ever remember Thee."

Powerful faith

In Puri, a saint who had completely dedicated himself to Lord Hari was seriously ailing from chronic dysentery. He became quite helpless and Lord Hari served him for months in the form of a servant. The law of karma is inexorable and no one can escape the operation of this infallible law. The Lord did not want His devotee to take another birth in order to exhaust his unalterable or *prarabdha karma*. So the saint had to suffer from the protracted ailment in order to purge his karma. But the Lord served him, as the saint had surrendered completely to Him. Look at the unbounded mercy of the Lord, who becomes a slave of His devotees when they depend upon Him entirely.

Self-surrender does not mean retiring to the forest or giving up all activities. *Tamas*, or inertia, is often mistaken for self-surrender. The ego and its desires have to be annihilated. The *rajasic* or dynamic mind is too obstinate to effect complete self-surrender. The lower nature repeatedly raises its head to assert itself and there is continual resurrection of desires. The desires are suppressed for some time and then manifest with redoubled force. Man is dragged hither and thither by these desires. Believe in divine possibilities and completely dedicate yourself to the Lord. Have full trust in Him and rest in peace. All cares, worries, anxieties, tribulations and egoistic efforts will terminate.

Look at the surrender and faith of Prahlada in God! He had completely resigned himself to Lord Hari. No other thought save that of God occupied his mind. He received the full grace and benediction of the Lord, even though he was ill-treated by his father in a variety of ways. He was hurled down from the top of a cliff, trampled by an elephant, and poisoned. Cobras were tossed upon him; he was thrown into the sea with his legs in iron chains. His nose was filled with poisonous gas; he was thrown into a fire and boiling oil was poured over his head. Yet Prahlada's faith in the Lord was not shaken in any way; the name of Narayana was always on his lips. Such must be the faith of every devotee.

The discipline of surrender to the Lord does not demand any special qualifications of culture, caste, birth, clan, sex, physical appearance, possessions or occupation. One who has dedicated everything of himself at the feet of the Lord and who constantly remembers Him succeeds in attaining God-consciousness. A saint rises above the three gunas. He has *para vidya*, the highest knowledge, through direct God-realization. He does not belong to any family or community, but to the whole of humanity. That is the reason why there is no social distinction among the saints.

The lower nature must be thoroughly overhauled. All old and inappropriate habits have to be destroyed, and then surrender becomes complete. Do not make plans and do not speculate. Keep the mind and the intellect passive. Allow the divine will and grace to work through your mind and senses. Become silent. Feel His grace and love, and enjoy the divine ecstasy. Be at ease. Pray fervently to God: "O Lord, make my will strong to resist all temptations, to control my senses and lower nature, to change my old unsuitable habits. Make my surrender complete and real. O Lord, enthrone Thyself in my heart. Do not leave this place even for a moment. Use my body, mind and organs as instruments. Make me fit to dwell in Thee forever."

Recognition and elimination of ego

Egoism, ambition and desire are obstacles in the way of self-surrender. Subtle, hidden desires will come to the surface of the mind. Any desires which are suppressed for some time will again manifest with doubled force if the aspirant is not careful, if there is some waning in his dispassion and spiritual practice, and if he mixes with worldly-minded people. Generally, the aspirant does not wish to part completely with his desires, and so consciously or unconsciously, willingly or unwillingly, keeps some desires for secret gratification. Therefore, the self-surrender is not perfect and unreserved, and so the grace of the Lord does not descend in its fullest measure. Even if there is an atom of desire or ego, it is not possible to receive the full measure of divine grace.

Complete surrender is when the devotee offers everything: mind, intellect, heart and soul, to his beloved Lord. The Lord becomes a slave to the devotee who has made absolute, ungrudging self-surrender, but if there is even a tinge of egoism, the Lord will not reveal Himself. Only after Surdas pricked his eyes with a thorn and remained without food and drink in a dense jungle did Lord Krishna appear before him with sweetmeats and water. When Draupadi was being disrobed, the Lord did not heed her cries as long as she still had traces of egoism. But He appeared upon the scene immediately when she cried out with total resignation: "O Krishna, O my beloved, come to my rescue!"

Renunciation of egoism is *sarva tyaga*, renunciation of everything. All desires, selfishness, attraction, repulsion and idea of the body depend on egoism. Egoism is the pivot or centre from which all these arise. When egoism is annihilated, surrender becomes complete. The self-arrogating little ego repeatedly persists and resists. It clings like a leech to its old habits, cravings and desires. It wages guerrilla warfare and resists surrender. It demands certain objects for its secret gratification. The vulgar, stiff, obstinate ego is harder than a diamond or steel, and it is very difficult to melt.

When one devotes one's life entirely to the Lord in order to fulfil the divine purpose of existence, one should not expect everything to happen in the way that one wants. Divine grace is not given for the fulfilment of your selfish needs. Constant vigilance and ceaseless effort are necessary to slay this dire enemy of peace and wisdom. Introspect and discover the subtle desires that lurk in the corners of the heart and mind, and then eliminate them ruthlessly through regular, silent meditation.

If one simply speaks the word surrender without real inner feeling, this will not constitute integral self-surrender. Surrender must come from the core of your heart, and once you surrender your personal and independent existence to God, your surrender is complete. Then you must be prepared for a radical change in your whole being and in the way in which you lead your life. You will become part of God and He will take care of your welfare as He sees fit. You will become a puppet of God and an instrument in His hands. Do not be too concerned with your body. God will save it if He needs it for further service. Surrender it at His feet and rest in peace. He will take care of it.

The real devotee says; "Let me take millions of births; it does not matter. However, let me be attached to the lotus feet of Lord Hari. Let me have spontaneous devotion to the Lord. Let me be endowed with purity, spiritual strength, selfless service and other divine virtues." Self-surrender is absolute devotion to God, and He wants your heart fully charged with pure love. There is no loss in total, unreserved self-surrender. It is not a bad bargain, rather it is a mighty gain indeed. A great transformation will come upon you; your little self will be dead. Your individual mind will merge into the cosmic mind, and all your ignorance will disappear.

The experience of samadhi
Self-surrender is the annihilation of individual consciousness and the attainment of absolute consciousness. When there is nothing but love of God and God-consciousness in the

devotee, then surrender becomes easy. The devotee becomes one with the Lord and loses his individuality. This is the law of being, the highest Truth. Here the soul rises through different states of consciousness until it attains absolute perfection and becomes unified with God. This is the culmination of all aspirations, all love and the highest devotion.

When the devotee surrenders, he merges himself in God; his mind merges in the Absolute. This is equal to *nirvikalpa samadhi*. The individual soul loses itself in the Supreme Self. The devotee becomes one with God. All worldly consciousness vanishes into universal consciousness. Man becomes God and the mortal becomes immortal. Absolute surrender gives immortality to man and he enters the kingdom of heaven on this earth itself. Whatever belongs to God becomes the possession of this highest devotee. All his karmas are destroyed and he no longer has any duties to perform. He is a perfected soul; he is the most blessed. The whole world appears to him as mere bliss. There is only the manifestation of supreme love everywhere.

This devotee has no sensual cravings or vanity for the body. He feels the presence of God and nothing else. He is fearless and has no anxieties, for everything is God and God is at all times everywhere with him. Whatever happens is the will of the Divine. He only wants to surrender, nothing else, because through absolute surrender he becomes totally saturated in the love of God. He becomes one with the universal consciousness and needs nothing more, for by attaining His grace he has attained everything. Nothing more can be added to his life. What is to be attained when God has bestowed His grace upon him?

In both the *Bhagavad Gita* and the *Srimad Bhagavatam*, innumerable verses state that surrender is the only way to attain the Supreme. Lord Krishna teaches Arjuna that self-surrender alone can give peace and relieve him of all his karma. Give up all ideas of duty and responsibility. Allow the divine will to work unhampered. This is the secret of surrender.

You will feel yourself to be a changed being. This exalted state is ineffable. A great transformation will come upon you. You will be enveloped in a halo of divine effulgence. You will be drowned in indescribable bliss, peace and joy. Your old little self will die. You will become a spiritual being. You will enjoy the immortal, divine life wherein there is neither despair nor fear, hunger nor thirst, doubt nor delusion.

Path of sadhana
Samarpan is complete surrender of the entire self to God, which makes the devotee feel the reality of divine grace and the Lord's readiness to help him at all times. The divine influence streams into his being and moulds it into a fit medium for divine realization and instrumentality. Surrender and grace are interrelated. Surrender draws down grace, and grace makes surrender complete. Surrender starts the purification of the heart and grace completes it. Divine grace destroys all impurities. Without grace, complete unification with God is not possible. Grace divinizes your being in order that the constant inflow of inspiration can be received and retained. It is through divine grace alone that the whole being is galvanized and rejuvenated.

You can realize the absolute or the impersonal God by surrender to the Divine. Surrender is not something to be done in a week or a month. You cannot totally surrender from the very beginning of your sadhana. The ego resists surrender and that is why Lord Krishna says: "Flee unto Him for shelter with all your being, O Bharata." The consciousness, ego, mind, intellect and soul should be placed at the feet of the Lord. Mira did this, and she obtained Lord Krishna's grace and became one with Him.

There is no loss in self-surrender; you get everything from the Lord. You enjoy all the divine attributes, *aishvarya*, of the Lord; the entire wealth of the Lord will belong to you. The *siddhis*, supernatural powers, and *riddhis*, highest delights, will roll under your feet. You will become one with the Lord. You will be freed from all wants, desires and cravings. The spiritually hungry and thirsty aspirant who yearns for the vision of the Lord turns towards the Divine. He is willing, eager and happy to consecrate his body, life, mind and soul to the feet of the Lord.

Self-surrender becomes perfect only after God-realization. The first stage is only a firm resolve to surrender oneself to God or to the preceptor. Renunciation of family life is the beginning of self-surrender. The aspirant who is endowed with burning *vairagya*, dispassion, and *viveka*, discrimination, and is really earnest will be able to surrender completely, even while living in the world. He will realize the Lord in and through the world by completely surrendering his entire being to Him. But very few are capable of this, because worldly life is beset with innumerable obstacles and temptations.

The aspirant finds it very difficult to attain complete dispassion in the midst of so many dissipations and distractions. Therefore, renunciation of family life makes his path easier and smoother. When the spiritual seed is sown, the aspirant goes to his preceptor and falls at his feet. Next the seed germinates. He starts to serve his guru. As his devotion increases and his service becomes sincere, his surrender becomes more perfect and complete. His heart becomes purer and purer, and gradually the light of knowledge dawns in him. Finally he recognizes the Supreme Atman, which pervades all, everywhere.

The actions performed by the sadhaka after renunciation do not bind him. As he offers all his actions to his preceptor or to the Lord, he does not perform any action which can be considered selfish. Thus, through service of one's preceptor with utter self-dedication, the heart becomes purified. Ultimately, the Lord becomes his preceptor, and in this way he completely surrenders himself to the Lord and attains the highest intuition. In the beginning individual effort is very necessary. But when surrender becomes complete, divine grace dawns in him and divine power does the sadhana for the sadhaka. The descent of divine grace and power take complete possession of his mind, will, life and body. The sadhana goes on with tremendous speed.

Through self-surrender the devotee becomes one with the personal form of God, just as the vedantic aspirant on the path of jnana yoga becomes one with the impersonal Absolute. Ultimately, the mind merges in the soul within and the sadhaka becomes a *jivanmukta*, a liberated sage. Sadhakas bold! The Lord loves you even when you turn away from Him. How much more will He love you if you turn to Him sincerely with faith and devotion! Very great is His love, greater than the highest mountains, very deep is His affection, deeper than the fathomless ocean! Make sincere efforts and behold the results of surrender.

2

Supreme Surrender

There are different views on bhakti, according to the moods or states of divine love which devotees experience, and their different stages of development or evolution. However, there cannot be any fundamental difference in the experience itself, in the essence of bhakti. All devotees unanimously agree on the essential characteristics of devotion, but some give prominence to particular indications.

In the *Srimad Bhagavatam*, Maitreya says that bhakti is a natural settling of the mind upon the highest Truth from which all objects and senses have come. In the *Narada Bhakti Sutras*, Sandilya describes bhakti as supreme love for God. In the *Devi Bhagavatam*, supreme love is compared to oil poured from one vessel into another; there is no break in the regular succession of thoughts about God. Kapila described devotion as a flow of uninterrupted thoughts towards God seated in the hearts of all beings, like the flow of the Ganga towards the sea. In the *Narada Panchatantra*, bhakti is spoken of as service rendered to the Lord through the senses, without being clouded by attachment, and purified by being directed towards Him. Sri Ramanujacharya identifies bhakti with loving meditation.

Devotion which is one continuous, unbroken stream of love for God and which is devoid of all taints is known as *mukhya bhakti*. Worship done without selfishness is *sattwic* devotion. Worship done to obtain power and wealth is *rajasic*, and worship done to injure others is *tamasic* devotion. Sattwa is stainless like crystal; however, it lays the trap of illusive happiness and knowledge, so it can be the golden fetter! A sattwic natured person, who compares himself with others and rejoices in his excellence, is puffed up with his knowledge and sure to fall. If his heart is filled with pride when it seems he has more comforts or more pleasant experiences, and if he thinks, "I am happy, I am wise," he is bound in the trap of illusion – caught! The attachment to his sattwic nature is an illusion.

Rajasic bhakti, which is practised in order to obtain power and wealth, is better than tamasic bhakti, which involves the invocation of divine help to injure others. Sattwic bhakti is still higher, for it only aspires to know God. A devotee should carefully watch his mind and note which of these conditions prevail. He should continually strive to increase sattwa and reduce rajas and tamas through satsang, japa, kirtan, meditation, worship, etc.

Surrender of the gopis

There are five main classifications of bhakti:
1. *Arta,* arising out of affliction
2. *Artharthi,* with self-interest
3. *Jignasu,* arising in the seeker of knowledge
4. *Mukhya,* liberated
5. *Para,* supreme.

The devotion practised by the seeker of truth, *jignasu*, is better than that practised by the seeker of wealth, *artharthi*. The devotion of the afflicted and the distressed, *arta*, is more fruitful than both of these types. An arta makes a passionate, sincere and intense appeal to the Lord and is given help immediately because he wants relief at once. His distress is due to conscious separation from God. An arta wants God and nothing else, because no one else can give him relief. A jignasu wants knowledge, not God. The artharthi does not want even knowledge; he wants wealth. Therefore, arta is best.

In the *Srimad Bhagavatam*, Narada mentions the gopis, the illiterate women of Vrindavan, as examples of the highest surrender. The gopis were artas; they were extremely miserable due to separation from Lord Krishna. They prayed and sang, and then the Lord gave them His presence. They played with Lord Krishna and identified themselves with Him with complete devotion. They cared not for family traditions, reputations or personal comforts, and lived in perfect devotion to Lord Krishna. They said: "Wherever we look, we find Shyama in the dark rain cloud, in the black pupils of our eyes, in the dark tamarind tree leaves, in the blue waters of the Yamuna and in the open sky."

When they heard the sweet, melodious flute of their beloved, they would leave their houses while milking the cows. They would rush to their lover with minds absorbed in Krishna, without even noticing each other's presence. Even if they were serving their husbands, they would leave them immediately. They would leave their household duties unfinished and run with their clothes and ornaments in disarray. When Krishna disappeared, they would ask the trees, the creepers, the earth and the deer if any of them had seen their beloved.

In the *Srimad Bhagavatam* (10:46), the Lord says: "The gopis have surrendered themselves heart and soul to Me. They think I am their life. They have abandoned all their closest relatives for My sake. I ever support those who cast aside all worldly pleasures for My sake." The love of the gopis was saturated with the knowledge of divine glory. They were God-intoxicated and unconscious of their earthly existence; they were drowned in the ocean of divine bliss. Their senses ceased to function and external objects did not produce any impression on their minds.

The gopis danced in the moonlight and played with Lord Krishna and yet they were conscious of His divinity, omniscience and omnipotence every second. They recognized Him as the soul of the universe and also as their own Atma. They surrendered themselves to Lord Krishna, knowing him to be God Himself and the embodiment of truth, consciousness and bliss. They said to Lord Krishna: "You are the primal *Purusha* or *Purushottam*, the Supreme Spirit, protector of the devas and the witness of everything. You have incarnated for the protection of the whole world."

The love of the gopis for the Lord cannot be adequately described in words. They dedicated their body, mind, intellect, wealth, youth, life and soul to the Lord. They always sang the Lord's glories with voices choked with emotion. They became restless and experienced acute agony in His absence, even if it was for a moment. The gopis surrendered all their actions at the lotus feet of Lord Krishna and were the crescent jewels among His devotees. They rejoiced in His glory; their happiness depended only on His happiness. Such was the indescribable state of the gopi's love. In the surrender of supreme devotion, the devotee sacrifices everything to the Lord and is willing to court even suffering for the His sake.

Exalted state of samarpan
The inner experiences of surrender are purely subjective and can be known only to the devotee himself. However, the characteristics or marks of surrender can be recognized. Every change in the heart finds external manifestations in the behaviour as well as appearance of the devotee. When a devotee is free from ego, desire and pain and beholds the Lord in everything, he feels that the world is a manifestation of the Lord, and all movements and actions are His *lila*, or play. He cannot detest anybody or anything. He feels that if he dislikes somebody, he dislikes the Lord Himself. He feels no loathing for scavengers, beggars, prostitutes or thieves, and says: "I see my sweet Lord everywhere; it is He who plays the role of prostitute, thief, dacoit or scavenger."

He experiences an all-embracing, all-inclusive, exalted mental state, which cannot be adequately described in words. This state is not intellectual; it is one of purest emotion, which has to be felt. Mira, Gauranga, Hafiz, Tulsidas, Kabir and Ramdas all enjoyed this state. Tulsidas says: "Knowing the whole world to be the manifestation of Sita and Rama, I prostrate to all with hands bowed in worship." In *Purusha Sukta* a similar description is found: "The Purusha, the Supreme Soul, has one thousand heads, one thousand eyes and one thousand feet." There is also an echo of this idea in the *Bhagavad Gita* (13:13): "With hands and feet everywhere, with eyes, heads and mouths everywhere, with ears everywhere, the Supreme Soul abides in the universe, pervading everything."

Lord Krishna offered Uddhava an easy way to reach Him: "Know, Uddhava, that the brahmin, chandala, ass, dog, king and beggar are all my forms. When you meet any object, prostrate and feel My presence." Nam Dev said to the dog, "O Vitala, my dear, in the form of a dog, do not run away with the dry bread. It will affect your soft throat. Pray let me apply ghee to it." He ran after the dog with the ghee in a cup. Sri Ramakrishna Paramahamsa prostrated before an outcast girl: "O Mother Kali, I see Thee in this girl!" Pravahari Baba prostrated before a thief holding a bag of stolen utensils: "O thief Narayana, pray accept these things. I never knew that thief Narayana was in my cottage." Ekanath gave his ring voluntarily to a thief who entered his house: "O thief, take this ring also. Thou art Krishna; your duty is to steal things. Keep up this lila."

A worldly person undertakes work for the pleasure or benefit derived from it, but no selfish work is done by a devotee who has surrendered to God. He is not attached to any person, object or place; he loves all, serves all and helps all. He is ever engaged in the good of all beings. He works for the enlightenment and upliftment of infant souls. Such a devotee does not promote his self-interest, but works for the good of all, without any sense of ego or feeling of external compulsion, in the spirit of service to God. As he is not prompted by ego he does not wish for fruits, so his actions are selfless and produce no karmas at all. He does not work for his personal pleasure and profit. He has no enthusiasm for selfish or worldly pursuits.

All weaknesses and faults vanish in the devotee who surrenders to God and serves Him and His creation. This devotee has no grief, because he has no particular attachment to any person or object. He expects nothing, hopes for nothing and fears nothing. How can darkness remain in the presence of light? How can sorrow arise in one who is immersed in the ocean of bliss and love? He has no disappointment, frustration, failure or loss. All these states are mental creations which manifest when the mind is attached to the body and illusory connections.

Darshan

Darshan, direct inner vision, of God comes in various ways: in dreams, in the physical form as an ordinary person, in the heavenly form with four hands holding a conch, mace, discus and lotus flower, in the form of cosmic consciousness, which Arjuna had, and in the form of supreme consciousness or full knowledge. In the *Bhagavad Gita* (11:19), Arjuna expressed his experience of cosmic consciousness as follows: "I see You without beginning, or middle or end; infinite in power, of endless arms, the sun and the moon being Your eyes, the sacrificial fire Your mouth, heating the whole universe with Your radiance."

The devotee who has surrendered himself to God is not affected by success or failure. When he has the fountain of all bliss by his side, how can there be any desire for the enjoyment of worthless and trivial sensual pleasure? He tastes the honey of divine love and so he does not depend on any worldly object for his personal satisfaction. How can a trace of earthly desire remain when God, the embodiment of bliss, is attained by the devotee? He does not desire or crave anything because he has no ego. He is filled with divine love and therefore feels no want. Desire exists only as long as the ego or the sense of separateness with its concomitant imperfections exists. When this state is transcended, all desires come to an end because their fulfilment is found in the Lord alone.

Nothing tempts the bhakta who has attained His love through total surrender. Just as a person who gets nectar to drink will not be tempted by cheap wine or muddy water, so also a devotee who has supreme love will not hanker after anything whatsoever. Compared to the invaluable treasure of divine love, the wealth of the three worlds appears to be a straw in the eyes of the bhakta, not to speak of sports cars, villas, name, fame or other worldly possessions. The sum total of all the pleasures of the universe is like a drop when compared to the ocean of bliss that is God, who is the source of all these pleasures.

When the bhakta is always immersed in the thought of God and sees Him alone in every thing and every being, how can he reject anybody or anything? When there is nothing greater than God, how can anything other than God cause elation in him? Grief results from attachment and desire. When the devotee does not desire anything, not even liberation, will he grieve for the loss of any possession? Instead, he will willingly renounce everything for the sake of attaining God and His love.

When a devotee who has surrendered to God performs any actions, it is God who acts through him. He is inwardly quite peaceful and serene when he serves the world out of love and mercy. When the devotee has attained eternal satisfaction in His love, the impulse to attain anything else disappears, and with it the desire to perform actions for the achievement of any personal gain. Only then can one be contented within oneself. There is no other gain superior to the absolute satisfaction attained through samarpan.

Intoxication of divine love

A devotee who has drunk the wine of divine love cannot observe the conventional rules of propriety. He is not a slave to the conventional laws of society and scriptures. The God-intoxicated devotee is not conscious of himself. The devotee grows into the likeness of the Lord and therefore shares His perfection with Him and partakes of His infinite bliss and joy. He has realized the Atman within and beholds the Atman in every creature. He becomes thoroughly intoxicated with divine love. He spends his days and nights singing the praises of the Lord and hearing about His glory. He remains merged in the Lord. He may laugh or weep or sing aloud or dance in divine ecstasy. Through the experience of bliss, he may also become silent and sit motionless like a statue. This is the state of identity or union with the Lord.

The devotee who has given himself to God loses his separate identity. He has no will of this own, as he has surrendered it completely to the Lord. He is simply an instrument in the hands of the God. St Francis of Assisi brought the marks of the crucifixion upon himself through intense meditation on Lord Jesus and joyfully experienced the extreme pain that Jesus had known. The Upanishads compare the Atman to honey; the Sufis often compare it to wine; the Shaktas compare it to liquor; and in vedic yajna it was called soma. All these symbolize the experience of the sweetness of divine bliss.

One who has been able to surrender everything becomes immortal. He lives in the presence of God; he is one with God and is able to commune with Him. He does not strive consciously for *mukti*, liberation, but God confers unsolicited liberation on His devotee. He has reached the source of everything and cares nothing for this world. He has no desires and so will take no further birth. Immortality constitutes the essential nature of this highest bhakta. He never feels the want of anything. Even *siddhis* or powers are worthless to him when compared to divine love. He does not care for them.

He enjoys supreme peace, eternal and perfect satisfaction, and ever-lasting bliss, and so becomes a *siddha*, a perfect man. He has reached the goal of life. He has attained God-realization. The sign of a perfect man, a siddha, is not the possession of miraculous powers, but the attainment of unity with the Supreme Being. He has realized the essence and totality of all and so is perfect, immortal and thoroughly satisfied. He cannot be distracted by external objects, which are incomplete, imperfect and only part of the whole.

Nothing can shake a person who rejoices in the Self, *atma rati*, who is satisfied in the Self, *atma tripta*, who is contented in the Self, *atma santushti,* and who plays in the Self, *atma krida*. When the devotee obtains the grace of God, his intellect is calm and tranquil. All the outgoing energies become transmuted into spiritual energy. He obtains help and strength from mantra, sadhana and upasana. Sattwa flows from the feet of the Lord towards his mind. He has firm, unshakeable conviction that real happiness is in God, and all his desires melt away. The distracting energy is destroyed and his mind becomes still and quiet. His senses no longer wander about; they become absorbed in the mind and the mind becomes absorbed in God. He is ever peaceful and delights in the bliss of God. Therefore, he is able to stand adamant amidst grave troubles and calamities. The devotee becomes serene and happy in the bliss of the Self.

The devotee who has surrendered to God has divine intoxication. When Lord Gauranga became intoxicated with the divine nectar of love, he sometimes did not know whether it was day or night. On one occasion, the young princess Mira danced in the streets amidst crowds of people when intoxicated by her love for Krishna. Sri Ramakrishna Paramahamsa often remained for days without food when he was intoxicated with divine love. Words cannot describe the nature of this divine intoxication. One has to feel it for oneself. Even if there is a mild intoxication, it will give the devotee immense strength with which to face all the difficulties in his sadhana.

Eleven forms of divine love

In the *Bhakti Sutras,* Devarishi Narada glorifies the path of devotion to the highest degree, as it is the path of absolute surrender to God, the eternal Truth. In the *Bhagavad Gita*, the bhakta is also given the highest place by Lord Krishna:

> Among all yogis, the one who, full of faith and with his inner self merged in Me, worships Me is deemed by Me to be the most devout. (6:47)

Those who, fixing their mind on Me, worship Me, ever steadfast and endowed with supreme faith, I consider to be the most perfect. (12:2)

Although surrender to God takes place through *bhakti* or divine love, each devotee will have a particular feeling of love or a relationship with God, which is characterized by a predominant attitude. Divine love manifests itself in the following eleven forms:
1. *Guna mahatmya shakti*: Love of glorification of the Lord's blessed qualities, such as those who delighted in singing His glories – Narada, Vyasa, Shukadeva, Kakabhusundi, Sesha, Suta, Saunaka, Sandilya, Bhishma, Prithu, Parikshit and Janamejaya
2. *Roopa shakti*: Love of His enchanting beauty, such as those who were naturally attracted by Lord Krishna's enchanting form – the gopis of Vrindavan and the rishis of Dadakaranya
3. *Pooja shakti*: Love of worship, such as those who spent their lives in worship – Ambarisha, Lakshmi, Prithu and Bharata
4. *Smarana shakti*: Love of constant remembrance – Prahlada, Dhruva and Shankara
5. *Dasya shakti*: Love of service, as a servant to his master – Hanuman, Akrura and Vidura
6. *Sakhya shakti*: Love of Him as a friend, a close personal relationship – Uddhava, Arjuna, Sudama and Guha
7. *Vatsalya shakti*: Love of Him as a child, with parental affection – Dasharatha, Kaushalya, Devaki, Nanda, Yashoda, Kasyapa, Aditi, Manu and Satarupa
8. *Kanta shakti*: Love for Him as a beloved wife or husband, where the remoteness disappears altogether and the two become one in spirit – Sridama, Rukmini and Satyabhama. In developing the bhava of kanta shakti the devotee must be careful not to be carried away by lustful propensities. The physical sensations of emotion are not devotion. A high standard of purity is required in those who take up this bhava, which is purely mental.

9. *Tanmaya shakti*: Love of complete absorption in Him – Sanat Kumar, Suka, Sanaka and Yajnavalkya
10. *Paramaviraha shakti*: Love felt in the utmost anguish of separation from the Lord – Uddhava, Arjuna, the gopis and Radha, when separated from Lord Krishna
11. *Atma nivedana shakti*: Love of total self-surrender, the highest manifestation of love with the feeling of constantly living in the presence of God anywhere and everywhere, where the devotee permanently loses himself in the Lord and becomes His instrument – Bali, Vibhishana, Hanuman, Ambarisha and Sibi.

These eleven types of bhakti are expressed during different moods. Most devotees develop one or two predominant sentiments and cultivate love for and surrender to God accordingly.

Surrender and humility

A devotee who surrenders to God and depends upon Him alone for everything in life develops communion with the Lord and is ever peaceful and blissful. Others depend upon their own self-efforts. In supreme devotion there is no room for pride in one's own efforts or spiritual discipline. There is not the slightest trace of ego. A devotee becomes an instrument in the hands of God and finds that He has always done everything for him. *Para bhakti* is absolute surrender or devotion, and that is why Krishna told Radha: "There are those who think themselves separate from Me. I rob them of their all, and when they see Me, all their ties to the world disappear. There are those who are worldly-minded, who kill the self in themselves. I play games with them until they forget all that is egoistic and selfish, and love Me for the sake of love alone, as you do, O Radha!"

God prefers humility to pride. Egoism is a great obstacle to the realization of God-consciousness. The more the ego is emptied, the more the heart will be filled with God. The grace of God is always there, but man's ego prevents him from receiving it. For those who are proud of their intellect, wealth, position, learning or birth, surrender to God is impossible. Mere verbal knowledge of God cannot develop devotion and give attainment of the supreme goal. An intellectual understanding of God is insufficient to attain the supreme goal of life. Bhaktas are humble, and humility is the foundation of bhakti yoga. Humility is the greatest of all virtues. All other virtues cling to a person who is endowed with humility.

Humility is the means to samarpan, and in this way it becomes the culmination of all sadhanas or disciplines. The hidden or unmanifest God is made manifest through devotion and humility. The devotee realizes that all is His will, and at this moment his surrender becomes complete. Devotion is the fruit of all sadhanas. Various disciplines such as raja yoga, religious rites, self-control, vows of various kinds, service to one's teacher and cultivation of divine virtues are described in the sacred scriptures, but devotion and surrender to the Lord is the end of them all. Purity of heart and annihilation of the ego is the result of karma yoga. *Kaivalya*, final liberation, is the fruit of raja yoga. *Jnana*, true knowledge and wisdom, is the fruit of the fourfold sadhana and self-inquiry. But the paths of jnana, karma and raja result in bhakti, devotion to the Lord, so bhakti is greater than all the other yogas.

3

Cultivation of Surrender

Surrender to God does not consist of believing in destiny; it is self-effort that draws the grace of God. One who lives a life of dullness cannot claim to have the radiant virtue of divine surrender. The idea that God inspires man towards virtue or vice, so what can he do by his own will, is backed up by ignorance. God is the indwelling reality in man. Therefore, one who adopts the path of self-effort by renouncing dependence on a fictitious destiny is able to draw upon the infinite resources of the Divine Self within. Only one who knows he is unable to live for a moment without the Lord, and remains engaged in devotional service by hearing, chanting, remembering, praying, worshipping and cultivating friendship with the Lord is able to surrender fully to the Lord. Such activities are auspicious and full of spiritual potency which make the devotee perfect in surrender, so that his only desire is to achieve communion with the supreme Lord.

One who controls the senses, who resorts to a great spiritual soul and serves him, and is free from the idea of 'I-ness' and 'mineness', will be able to completely surrender to God. Such a devotee undoubtedly approaches the Lord without difficulty. In the *Bhagavad Gita* (10:10), Lord Krishna says: "To those who are constantly devoted to serving Me with love, I give the knowledge by which they can come to Me." By the mercy of the Lord, such a devotee never comes back to the material condition of life. The Lord helps this devotee to achieve Self-realization through yoga, and when he becomes fully established in God-consciousness, He protects him from falling down into conditioned life again.

Do not waste a moment

In the *Bhakti Sutras*, Devarishi Narada says that when one has given up pleasure and pain, desire and gain, and is in a state of high spiritual expectancy, not even half a moment should go by in vain. Time free from the sway of pleasure, pain, desire, profit or other worldly considerations is what every spiritual aspirant seeks. Therefore, every second should be spent in meditation on God. Happiness is the quality of sattwa, sadness of tamas and desire of rajas. When one has given up pleasure, sadness and desire, the qualities of the three gunas, and is waiting for the appearance of the Lord, even half a second should not be wasted.

One needs to be extremely alert because the mind can wander within an instant. God may come and go without one noticing Him. All aspirants are ever prone to their instinctive tendencies and if one is not vigilant and alert, rajas and tamas will destroy any progress made on the path. One should be ever watchful for God's appearance, as time is most precious. In youth, one is enveloped in darkness. In adolescence, one is carried away by lust and given to sexual pleasure. In old age, one groans under the burden of samsara. Much time is spent in sleep, vain discussions and idle gossip. Another portion of life is spent in disease and suffering. Where then is the time for virtuous actions and divine contemplation? Life is uncertain, so a wise person is careful to spend his time in spiritual pursuits and service of God, with an attitude that promotes the growth of devotion and surrender.

The principles of *yama* and *niyama*, ethical codes of conduct, are very important here. No spiritual progress is possible without these disciplines. Virtues like non-violence, truth, purity and faith in the existence of God have to be developed. Practice of these virtues purifies the heart and prepares the mind for the reception of divine light. Compassion softens the hard heart. Truth purifies the heart. God is an embodiment of truth and can be reached through the practice of truthfulness alone. Truth alone triumphs. If one is well-established in the practice of non-violence in thought, word and deed, all other virtues will cling to him. Most vicious actions are performed in anger. *Brahmacharya*, sensual restraint due to attraction to the divine, is the highest of all virtues. Without brahmacharya, there will be no realization. Without faith in God, neither sadhana nor realization is possible. Faith is the fundamental qualification of an aspirant. This is not blind faith, but faith based on experience and reason.

Devarishi Narada points out the need to have reverence for the ideal of highest surrender and the divine qualities necessary to attain this state, such as courage, charity, austerity, straightforwardness, humility, self-abnegation, tranquillity, freedom from anger, tenderness of heart, sobriety, forgiveness and fortitude. All the practices enjoined by the scriptures are only to remove the ego or veil of ignorance. The bhakta concentrates his mind completely on God without a break. In fact, his whole heart, body, intellect and soul is given to God without any reservation.

Every act that elevates the mind and awakens the feeling of surrender must be performed. Keep the pooja room clean, decorate it, light a lamp and burn incense. Bathe, wear clean clothes and apply bhasma and kumkum to the forehead. Wear a rudraksha or tulsi mala. All these simple actions have a benign influence on the mind and generate devotion. They help to create the necessary *bhava*, or inner feeling, to invoke the deity that you want to worship. As a result the mind will be easily concentrated.

Practise right conduct, attend satsang, practise mantra japa, remember the Lord, sing kirtan, pray, worship, serve the saints, reside in places of pilgrimage, serve the poor and the sick with divine feeling, offer all actions and their fruits to the Lord, feel the presence of the Lord in all creation, prostrate before the image of God and saints, renounce earthly enjoyments and wealth, give charity, perform austerities and vows, practise non-violence, truth and restraint of the senses. All these will help to develop devotion and surrender to God.

Satsang, japa and kirtan

By keeping the company of mahatmas and saints, one develops dispassion and discrimination and no longer prefers the company of worldly people. The mind becomes steady and one-pointed, free from delusion and infatuation, and rests in the essence. Those who practise what they preach are the only teachers fit to teach about surrender. They move along the path about which they speak. Their teaching alone will be most effective, as they actually live a life of surrender to the Lord. Acharyas or teachers are those who have had first-hand experience of spiritual disciplines and their consequent realization.

The Lord's name uttered knowingly or unknowingly burns up sins, just as fire burns fuel. One who does kirtan and japa of the Lord's name derives the merit from all austerities, sacrifices, baths in sacred waters and study of the Vedas. Kirtan and japa of the divine name enter into the heart and bring all sorrows and miseries to an end. Therefore, these practices are surely the supreme method for the attainment of devotion and surrender. Japa and kirtan are very helpful in meditation, self-purification and realization. The aspirant may reach the highest samadhi by these methods. Successful japa results in restraint of mind, purity, silence and freedom from distraction. Mantra generates special vibrations in the body, mind and atmosphere, which are highly beneficial for spiritual practice.

Man undergoes miseries and sufferings because he has forgotten God due to the influence of ignorance or illusion. The devotee in whom His grace descends can never forget Him. Try to remember the Lord with every breath. Always keep the *Bhagavad Gita* in your pocket and a japa mala around your neck. Repeat His name always, instead of allowing mundane thoughts to dominate your mind. Be in the company of bhaktas. Study the *Srimad Bhagavatam, Ramayana* or *Bhagavad Gita* every day. Then you cannot forget Him.

Reduce your wants. Do not try to fulfil desires as they spring up in your mind. Devote one day to mantra japa. Do japa *anushthana* or prescribed sadhana during the Easter, Christmas and summer holidays. Join *akhanda* or continuous kirtan for several days, eating only fruits and milk, wearing simple clothes and observing *mouna*, silence, during breaks. Observe perfect mouna and celibacy. Then there is no possibility of forgetting Him, as the Lord will be ever close to you. The Lord says: "O Narada, I dwell not in Vaikuntha, nor in the hearts of yogis, but wherever my bhaktas sing my name."

Service to saints is known as *seva* and enables one to develop devotion to God. A saint is the supreme refuge for those who are immersed in the formidable ocean of worldly existence. Worldly attachments and sins are easily got rid of through service to saints.

Overcoming the attraction of desires

There can be no surrender in the mind until it is freed from all cravings. The feeling of 'I' and 'mine' in everything you do and deal with is the strongest of all attachments. Renunciation of worldly objects forms the cornerstone of all spiritual discipline. One enjoys supreme bliss and peace through renunciation of objects of enjoyment, because sensual pleasures cause distraction in the mind. They weaken the will and render the mind unfit for concentration and divine contemplation. They generate cravings and destroy discrimination, dispassion, devotion and the power of enquiry into the nature of the ultimate Truth.

Sensual cravings correspond to the five sense organs: sound, touch, sight, taste and smell. If there is any craving when objects are renounced, the surrender is not true or complete. So leave all cravings; this is real surrender of the ego. One can overcome the attraction to objects of desire by uninterrupted worship of God. There are many trials on the path of devotion, such as disease, loss and frustration. The devotee should bear them all with great patience. In the *Bhagavad Gita* (8:14), Lord Krishna says: "I am easily attainable by that ever steadfast yogi who constantly and daily remembers Me (for a long time), not thinking of anything else (with a one-pointed mind)."

No one can cross this formidable ocean of birth and death without some form of ceaseless worship of the Lord. All service to the Lord in a spirit of divine bhava is defined as *upasana*, worship. *Seva*, service to humanity, and *pooja* are forms of worship. To hear about the Lord, to sing His names and glories, to remember Him, to do His service, to worship Him with flowers, to surrender to Him all works done, to offer the body to His service and care are all forms of upasana. The *para bhakta* or supreme bhakta considers even eating and sleeping, walking and talking as acts of worship of the Lord. He does not separate divine and ordinary life.

Even while engaged in daily life, all activities may be turned into upasana by constant remembrance of the Lord with divine bhava. Therefore, always maintain the right mental attitude during any work. Feel that it is the Lord within you who eats, sleeps, etc., and the ego will be completely effaced. That is absolute surrender to the Lord. To surrender in totality you must become an undaunted spiritual aspirant, unafraid of any obstacles or difficulties that may come your way. You must surmount each obstacle patiently and cross all the hurdles that stand in your spiritual path. Let the inner spiritual fire and aspiration burn steadily. Plod on, persevere and emerge victorious. Yield not to weakness and temptation. Be vigilant, be on the alert. Kill negligence, sloth and carelessness.

Rest by changing your work. Doing kirtan will give you the necessary rest and remove fatigue. Create interest in your spiritual practices through a variety of methods, such as mantra writing, japa, kirtan, chanting, prayer, meditation, study and service. All these will focus your awareness on God.

The devotee needs to be very vigilant and cautious, and that is why Lord Krishna says (8:7): "O Arjuna, always remember Me alone and at the same time carry out your prescribed duties. With your activities dedicated to Me and your mind and intelligence fixed in Me, you will attain Me without doubt."

Regular, unbroken upasana for an extended period will take you to your goal, whereas worship in bits and pieces, now and again, will not produce any substantial experience. Upasana must be constant, like a flow of oil. If there is any break, desires will enter your mind. Worldly thoughts and temptations will capture your ego. Old desires will be resurrected and new ones created. Maharishi Patanjali says in the *Yoga Sutras* (1:14): "*Abhyasa,* spiritual practice, becomes established when it is carried out ceaselessly, with reverence and zeal, for a long time."

Solitude and sadhana

Inner solitude is essential for sadhana and surrender. It is an aid in rooting out the binding force of worldly attractions and temptations. A solitary place is one where the din and noise of sensual desires and cravings for sensual objects do not penetrate. Merely retiring to a forest is of little spiritual value. One who has cravings and desires meets temptations, even in a forest. A solitary place, like an ashram that is centred on service to humanity, is favourable for the practice of detachment and dispassion. An aspirant must live there without the comforts and objects he likes best, because he cannot obtain them.

When one lives in solitude for a considerable period, social ties automatically slacken. One's own heart is the most secret, lonely and sacred place for meditation. However, loneliness is not advisable for all. Many become lazy, depressed and unclean if they live in seclusion. An aspirant can exhaust his karmic attachments and develop ethical virtues only by remaining in the world. The world is the best teacher. Only advanced sadhakas can remain in seclusion for extended periods and be benefited.

Sadhana is spiritual practice in order to transcend the three gunas. *Sattwa guna* is the enlightening quality; it is of the nature of light and harmony. *Rajas guna* is the inflaming quality, the nature of passion and motion. *Tamas guna* is the enveloping or obscuring quality, the nature of inertia and darkness. These are the forces of maya that bind the soul to the world. *Maya* is the illusory power of God which takes you away from reality and attracts you to the fleeting, sensual pleasures. The working of maya is very subtle and difficult to detect. The aspirant must be very vigilant, because the strongest attachment is to the ego, which binds one to the play of the gunas and must be cut asunder.

In the spiritual sense *yoga* means union with God, God-realization, or the practice of yoga sadhana or discipline through which God is realized. *Kshama* means maintaining one's progress on the path of God-realization, and refers to the merciful protection of the Lord. When the devotee depends entirely upon God and is ever united with Him, the Lord Himself looks after his yoga and kshama. However, a devotee should not give up his spiritual practice or social service at any stage, either before or after realization.

The devotee who feels that he is an instrument in the hands of God renounces all sense of doership and agency. Whatever he does is for the sake of the Lord. He does not expect any reward for his actions. Further, he has no attachment to karma or its fruits. When the devotee totally surrenders, God destroys his ego and begins to act through his organs. Now the devotee is freed from the pairs of opposites. Selfish actions have no attraction for him. One who conquers the pairs of opposites really conquers the whole world, because the world is a play maintained by the pairs of opposites, which affect the mind through the mental currents of attraction and repulsion. Therefore, one who transcends always keeps a balanced mind, which is an important sign of a *jivanmukta* or liberated soul.

As the devotee advances, he becomes merged in the Lord. Although he does not deliberately renounce the Vedas, their influence is reduced as he has realized the goal of life. A realized man does not need the rituals prescribed by the Vedas, but they are useful in earlier stages as a means for God-realization. The Vedas are of no interest to one who has surrendered to God and experiences an incessant flow of divine love. He is above the injunctions imposed by them. His love for God is not diluted by desires of any kind. The love that arises at this stage is never satisfied until God is realized. This love is *mukhya bhakti*, one-pointed devotion to God for His own sake. The lower stage of bhakti is love of God for a particular purpose.

Abstention from argument and discussion
The duty of the devotee is to remember God every second, without the need for argument or criticism. He need not know how, when or why the world was created as God will reveal this truth to him whenever He wills. The devotee need not enter into argumentation or vain discussions regarding the existence or attributes of God, as the true spirit of enquiry vanishes with this type of discussion and the joy of intellectual gymnastics or verbal warfare takes its place. God is realized through purity of mind and meditation, not by vain discussions. That is why in the *Kathopanishad* Lord Yama says to Nachiketas: "This Atman cannot be obtained by too much learning, discussion or intelligence." One who is chosen by the Lord receives the vision of the Atman by the grace of God. To him alone the Lord manifests Himself and reveals His nature. The duty of a devotee is to surrender to God and to realize God. Love is above reasoning.

Argumentation is a great hindrance on the path of surrender because it produces unnecessary agitation, and an agitated mind cannot grasp the truth. Vain discussions about God must not be encouraged, as they can continue indefinitely. Every topic relating to God can be argued in a variety of ways and such endless discussions will not lead to any definite or positive conclusions. Mere reasoning does not lead to realization of God, as the intellect is finite and unable to grasp the infinite. None of the great problems which affect human life have ever been conclusively solved by reasoning. The devotee does not depend on reasoning, but on intuition, which is infallible and correct. For the attainment of surrender, one should give up heated discussions, be humble, and perform practical sadhana. Do not waste time and energy in vain argumentation.

Spiritual study
The teachings of scriptures that promote spiritual dedication should constantly be meditated upon and actions that rouse devotion should be performed. A devotee should study books which place the ideals of devotion before him: the glory, sweetness and lilas of the Lord, stories of saints and practices which help to cultivate surrender. The most important books on devotion are the *Ramayana, Srimad Bhagavatam, Bhagavad Gita, Narada Bhakti Sutras, Vishnu Purana, Vishnu Sahasranam, Sandilya Sutras, Shiva Purana* and *Devi Bhagavatam*. Devotion develops by studying such devotional scriptures. The saints say that these scriptures are invested with the power to transform the heart of humanity.

The devotee must not be lenient with the mind. In this respect, following all the guidelines described in the bhakti shastras will prevent laziness and worldliness overtaking. The benefits of following a daily routine and maintaining a spiritual diary will constantly uplift the thoughts and actions. In every aspect of life, in all the modes and moods of existence, pure devotees have only God-consciousness. In their attitude to members of their family, to their friends who do good and to those who do evil, to their superiors and inferiors, in every relationship that exists between them and others, they have only consciousness of God.

Perfection and surrender
Devotion to God secures freedom from the wheel of birth and death. The devotee who surrenders to God attains immortality and lives constantly in the presence of God.

Immortality, supreme peace, absolute consciousness, eternal bliss, unbroken joy, nirvana, freedom and perfection are synonymous terms for God, and can only be attained by devotion and surrender to God. Worldly pleasure is not constant. One may smile and laugh for five minutes, but he will weep bitterly later. Even a billionaire is full of cares, worries, anxieties and fear lest he lose his wealth. Everyone wants eternal happiness, infinite knowledge, immortality, freedom and independence, but these are obtained only through *samarpan*, total self-surrender. How can we surrender to God whom we have not seen? The scriptures and teachers have recommended the following ways:

1. Remain in the company of bhaktas and saints
2. Listen to stories about God, His divine powers, grace and beauty
3. Sing His names daily and practise mantra japa
4. Serve bhaktas and saints
5. Visit and reside in places of pilgrimage.

The bhakta achieves perfection through surrender to God. He sees God in all, and all in God. Therefore, he ceases to perform actions of his own volition. A similar idea is expressed in the *Bhagavad Gita* (12:17): "One who neither rejoices, nor hates, nor grieves, nor desires, who renounces both good and evil, and who is full of devotion, is very dear to Me." This pure devotee becomes the instrument of God and performs actions without desire or attachment, in accordance with His will for the well-being of the whole world.

When one has surrendered to God, everything in life becomes natural, effortless and automatic. Life itself is the flow of divine will. God sometimes gives darshan to encourage His devotees. However, the devotee should not stop his sadhana when he receives darshan. He should ever rest in God and continue his spiritual practices until he naturally merges himself in the Lord. Spiritual effort is necessary as long as the ego or feeling of separateness persists. When these are removed and when the light of the Divine has descended into the devotee, he puts forth no more effort. This is confirmed by the Lord in the *Bhagavad Gita* (2:59): "The sense objects turn away from one who restricts sense enjoyment, although the taste remains. But on experiencing the highest state, fixed in Supreme Consciousness, all sensory longing ceases."

Absolute surrender is not limited by any considerations of caste, creed, colour, sex or country. Every human being who has faith, devotion and aspiration can cultivate samarpan through supreme love and attain God-realization. The Puranas speak even of animals receiving the grace of the Lord. Therefore, attain that love of God in this very birth, in this very instant! All your sorrows, desires, cravings, fears and anxieties will end. You will become perfect and enjoy eternal satisfaction. You will be immersed in perennial bliss.

4

Preparation and Qualifications

An aspirant cannot attain *samarpan*, absolute surrender, without preparation and proper qualifications. Ramanuja, the founder of the Vishishta Advaita school of philosophy, mentions seven qualifications as being indispensable for those who wish to follow this path.
1. *Viveka*: discrimination
2. *Vimoha*: freedom from desires
3. *Abhyasa*: spiritual practices
4. *Kriya*: the habit of doing good to others
5. *Kalyana*: purity in thought, word and deed, non-violence, charity and other virtues
6. *Anavasada*: cheerfulness
7. *Anuddharsha*: absence of excessive hilarity.

Some other qualities required on this path are: aspiration, faith, tolerance, patience, perseverance, mercy, serenity, cheerfulness, courage, non-violence, truthfulness, purity, moderation, spirit of selfless service, dispassion, renunciation and a one-pointed mind. The aspirant should have faith in the grace of God and an intense desire to attain God-realization. He must have deep faith in the scriptures and in the spiritual teacher. He must have the capacity to understand. He must be free from disabilities and have every possible opportunity and favourable circumstances. Only then will he be fit for the path of surrender; only then will he be benefited. In order to attain surrender, the aspirant must strive for the love of God alone. Sincere efforts must be made to obtain His grace. Only those practices that enable one to obtain His grace should be adopted. In order to cultivate divine love, the necessary actions must be performed to obtain it. Through the grace of God, surrender will happen. That alone is valuable in the life of an aspirant; everything else is of no value. His grace must be obtained. The methods have already been given: detachment, selfless service, kirtan, hearing the Lord's lilas, and so on. If one trusts in God, there is no need to ask anything of Him; He gives everything without asking.

Devotion is the main requisite of surrender and covers a wide range of virtues: selflessness, egolessness, fellowship, amity, forgiveness, compassion and love. A true devotee is patient, humble, unselfish, honest, faithful, kind, and absolutely pure. Finally, we are given the promise that a true devotee who surrenders everything to God will be brought face to face with our Lord. The two salient virtues which stand out most clearly are kindness and purity. Next to these is the constancy of love that never fails. Love is kind; a loving person must be kind. Kindness is the very essence of love. To be kind is to be compassionate and forgiving, gentle and sweet, sympathetic and understanding, and ready to help anyone in need. Kindness constitutes not only the positive things that one thinks, says and does, but also those things one does not think, say or do. One can be kind by not passing on that unkind remark heard about a friend or by not saying that thoughtless and tactless word that was on the tip of the tongue.

Purity is a most important requisite. In order to love God with all of one's heart and soul, throughout all one's days, one must have pure thoughts and always act in pure ways. Nothing but the best motives must be attributed to other people. One's every thought must be holy, unselfish and in accordance with God's will, then one has purity. A devoted person thinks no evil. Absolute purity is thinking no evil at all, not even a single evil thought. How divinely pure! His every thought is holy and unselfish and in accordance with God's will. What a glorious ideal!

Faithfulness must also be included, faith that never fails. Love that never lets you down is based on faith. One who has faith and truly loves will never let you down. If we have faith in others, we should never let them down. The Lord's love is constant and never fails; it is the one thing that can be completely relied upon. True love is faithful, loyal, devoted, constant and never fails. The devotee with such love is assured of the complete fulfilment of all that is hoped for. His doubts will be cleared; all that is not understood will be made clear. There will be no more separation, for he will be united with God.

Easiest way to surrender
Devotion is the direct approach to surrender through the heart. Devotion is the easiest form of spiritual practice because love is natural to everybody. Devotion can be practised under all conditions and by all alike, irrespective of age and sex. Learning, austere penance, study of the Vedas and a brilliant intellect are not needed for the attainment of devotion. What is wanted is constant and living remembrance of God, coupled with faith. That is the reason why the path of bhakti is available to everyone. Many people think poorly of bhakti yoga and prefer to take up the practices of hatha yoga, kundalini yoga or raja yoga, without the necessary preparations, such as yama and niyama. They think they can move along the spiritual path without devotion to God, and misunderstand what God-realization is. They imagine that it is the attainment of miracles, such as the ability to walk on water or fly through the sky.

Karma yoga, raja yoga and jnana yoga are only stepping stones to knowledge and devotion, but they purify the heart of the aspirant. Of these three paths, raja yoga is beset with the most difficulties and dangers. The raja yogi attains powers, then misuses them and has a downfall. In hatha yoga it is very difficult to practise asana, pranayama and pratyahara correctly. In jnana yoga the pursuit of knowledge is dry for some, while the path of bhakti yoga or devotion is sweet and enjoyable. Jnana yoga demands vast study, a sharp and subtle intellect, bold understanding and gigantic will. Bhakti yoga demands only love and bestows everything: siddhis, the grace of God and darshan without difficulty.

In the path of devotion there is no need for any other evidence, as proof of devotion is devotion itself. The devotee has direct experience of divine bliss when he is in communion with the Lord. There is no need for any external proof. Bhakti is not something to be verbally explained; it deals with direct recognition of the emotion of love. There is no need for any external proof when one loves a mother, wife or child because love is a direct experience. Intellectual arguments are not required. Any amount of argument cannot convince one about one's own experience or feeling. Direct experience is the primary and infallible means of all valid knowledge.

The path of devotion leads to supreme peace and bliss. The devotee lives only for God, in God, and forgets everything else, even himself. His love of God is experienced as supreme peace and bliss. The devotee need not entertain any anxious thoughts, as he has consecrated himself completely to the Lord. He need not worry if his affairs go wrong, because his entire life has been surrendered to the Lord. He maintains complete trust in God, even when his affairs appear to be going the wrong way. The devotee surrenders himself as well as his temporal and spiritual concerns to the Lord, so he need not worry about worldly losses. When the devotee has surrendered himself as well as his all to the Lord, the Lord removes all his anxieties. He takes away the mind of His devotee.

The path of surrender does not advocate hardness of heart or indifference to human suffering. It does not condemn the charitable acts and philanthropic work of large-hearted people. It emphasizes that the devotee has no need to entertain any anxiety or worry regarding worldly matters. He surrenders his soul, intellect, mind and body. He surrenders all his attachments to the world along with his reverence for the scriptures and all the spiritual disciplines and rules. He offers everything to the Lord, and in return the Lord makes him His own.

Direct all emotions to God

The devotee who entirely depends on God can make Him the object of his passion, anger and pride. Just as the Lord may be the object of love for His devotee, He may also be the object of his desire, anger and frustration. No one exists except the Lord in the eyes of the devotee, so who else will become the object of these other emotions and feelings? All our internal and external feelings should become a sacred offering unto the Lord. Only then will they be transmuted and welded into pure devotion or bhakti. Devarishi Narada tells the bhakta that: "Having once dedicated all activities to God, he should show his desire, anger, egoism etc. only to Him."

In this manner, the emotions which stand as obstacles on the spiritual path are changed into aids when directed towards God. Pride, passion and anger become absorbed in the Lord. If the devotee is angry, he is angry at his beloved; if he is proud, he is proud of the Lord; if he has a desire, his Lord alone is the object of that desire. Persistent thinking of the Lord, whether in love or hatred, transforms the heart into a sacred shrine. Ravana hated Lord Rama, but he attained a high state after his death because his mind dwelt constantly on the Lord.

Anger may also be directed towards the obstacles to devotion. In this way it will take the form of dispassion and renunciation. When one directs anger towards his own malevolent qualities, he purifies himself. The evil impressions will vanish and the sattwic nature will manifest fully.

What to observe and avoid

The ordinary way of life should not be given up until bhakti is achieved, but renunciation of the desire for reward should be persistently practised. Conscious efforts must be made continuously to perform selfless work and cultivate mental discipline. One must eat, breathe and act throughout life, so there is no excuse to give up the duties entrusted to one. Rather, love should be cultivated in the form of constant service of the Lord, *dasya bhava*, or constant devotion to the Lord, like that of a devoted wife, *kantabhava*.

In the *Bhakti Sutras* Devarishi Narada says: "One must not neglect to observe social customs and ceremonies until bhakti is developed. One should continue to perform one's duties, but the fruits of these activities should be surrendered to the Lord." Contributing towards the upliftment of society should not be given up upon the attainment of bhakti, or even for the attainment of it. All beneficial activities must be continued; only the fruits of such actions must be relinquished. Sri Vasishtha, Sri Vyasa, Sri Shankaracharya, Lord Jesus, Lord Buddha and others have been most active benefactors of mankind, and are perfect examples to follow.

All the scriptures advise the aspirant to give up all worldly entertainments, gossip, attitudes and company which decrease spirituality and render the devotee incapable of further progress. One whose mind is engrossed in thoughts of the opposite sex can never meditate on God. Such thoughts arouse passion, and passion is the greatest obstacle on the path of God-realization. Thoughts of wealth generate greed. The thoughts and company of an atheist destroy one's faith in God and cause disbelief in God to arise. The thought of an enemy generates anger. The thought of and association with wealthy people induces thoughts of luxury in the mind. Therefore, these types of thoughts and associations should be avoided.

The aspirant must avoid immoral company everywhere, at all times and by all means. A neophyte who keeps company with immoral people loses his devotion and develops contemptuous qualities. He quickly returns to the level of the worldly person because the human mind imitates and is greatly influenced by the company it keeps. The aspirant will grow in spirituality and virtue if the food, associations, topics of discussion, environment, vocation, form of worship and books read are sattwic. If they are rajasic or tamasic, one will develop those traits. Worldly company is the main obstacle to devotion.

In the company of the impious, one develops immorality, licentiousness, vicious habits, voluptuousness, sensuality, hypocrisy, arrogance, and so on. Such company destroys all the virtues, such as purity, truthfulness, love and compassion. Some people argue: "Why should malevolent company be avoided; is God not there too? Why should evil be seen anywhere; should one not see only the good? Should we not see only God in evil also?" A sage alone is above good and evil. He alone is able to clearly perceive good in the immoral. For him there is neither good nor evil. He alone will not be affected by evil because he is truly able to see God in all. Decadent company will easily affect ordinary people and especially an aspirant, because vice is still a solid reality.

God is everywhere, but when the aspirant is in the midst of temptations, he cannot take refuge in the upanishadic saying: "All indeed is Brahman." Every object that stimulates lower passions must be ruthlessly avoided. Sublime instructions that lead to the attainment of God-realization or eternal bliss should only be imparted to the aspirant who is endowed with purity, discrimination and dispassion, and who is free from cravings for sensual pleasures. For they alone will hear what is being said and try to act accordingly.

Worldly-minded people may talk of pleasurable worldly experiences and attractive objects they have seen. A novice on the spiritual path, or even a spiritually advanced soul who has not yet attained self-realization, who is not rooted in the conviction of the utterly illusory nature of the world, will be impressed by such experiences and may turn away from the spiritual path and desire to join them. The natural tendency of the mind is to be attached to something. The mind is normally attached to objects. If this tendency is to be annihilated, it must be turned towards God or the Atman. The aspirant must have faith in and devotion for God. He must have intense aspiration and dispassion, lead a contented life and possess the three fundamental virtues: *ahimsa,* non-violence, *satyam,* truth, and *brahmacharya,* continence. It is essential that he should be free from crookedness, cunningness, diplomacy, double-dealing, harshness, rudeness, greed and egoism. He should be gentle, humble and noble.

The aspirant has to adopt the golden medium, observe moderation in everything and lead a well regulated and disciplined life of self-restraint. He must gradually discipline the senses and keep them in subjugation. He should possess a loving heart and never injure the feelings of others, even in jest. He must not be jealous of the prosperity of others or compare his privileges with those of others. Without the spirit of selfless service and self-restraint, it is impossible to surrender to God.

The aspirant must speak truthfully. He must not use vulgar or harsh words. He should always be content, earnest, vigilant and diligent. He must possess adaptability, courage, mercy, generosity, tolerance, patience, perseverance and discrimination. He should bear insult and injury, and have equanimity, fortitude and forbearance. He must have mannerliness. His speech must agree with his thoughts and his actions must agree with his speech. Boasting, back-biting and laziness should have no place. He should never miss introspection and self-analysis, even for a single day. He must stick to his ideal and be ever aware of his goal. He should make a point of practising one virtue at a time, and do at least one good action every day.

Love transcends all base emotions

Devotion or bhakti that seeks to serve and love without any motive whatsoever should always be the ideal of a devotee. A loyal servant or a devoted wife does not expect any return or even gratitude from the master or the husband for all the services rendered as an offering of love. Even so, the highest bhakta sees only God in every creature. All his activities will therefore take the form of an offering of pure love to the

Lord, without any selfish motive or even recognition from Him. He loves because he cannot help loving God.

The bhakta who is exclusively attached or devoted to the Lord is considered to be the best of His devotees. His body, mind, wealth and everything else become the property of God. He lives in the world as His instrument with his mind ever absorbed in God. His eyes see the Lord everywhere, at every moment. The Lord settles in the eyes of the devotee, and no one else can enter his eyes. Even sleep has no access there. One who attains this absolute state of devotion is called a *bhagavata*, a saint.

This primary devotion is not tinged with any worldliness or selfishness. The devotee does not long for *mukti*, liberation. He does not love God as a means to an end. A description of the nature of such a bhakta is given in the *Srimad Bhagavatam*: "He who has resigned his mind to me does not seek the position of Brahma or that of Indra, or an emperor's throne or lordship over Patala, or the attainment of yogic powers, or even moksha from which there is no returning; for he desires nothing but Myself."

That is the nature of ekanta bhakti. *Ekanta* means 'having only one end'. That end is to be in communion with the Lord, always and ever in His service, having fully surrendered to Him. Such devotees have realized that His will is everything.

5

The Four Jewels

Samarpan, absolute self-surrender, is not a subject that can be understood and realized by mere intellectual study, reasoning, rationalization, discussions or arguments. It is actually the most difficult of all paths. Mere scholarly erudition and vast study with a high degree of intelligence alone cannot help one in the practical realization of this state of consciousness. It demands total renunciation of one's ego, a discipline that is not to be found in the studies offered by modern universities and colleges. It requires no less than the total commitment and dedication of one's entire being. In order to live in the state of samarpan, in communion with the Divine, one has to reach that realm where is there is neither darkness nor light, East nor West, gain nor loss. This realm can never be reached by either the mind or the senses.

Samarpan is not an imaginary region from the *Arabian Nights* or *A Midsummer Night's Dream*. It is not an illusory place of mythological fabrication. It is the one and only real, everlasting abode of perennial peace and deep, abiding joy, wherein this fluctuating restless mind can find permanent rest. Sages like Shankara, Dattatreya, Mansoor, Madalsa, Gargi, Chudali and others have reached this destination after strenuous struggle and exertion. The aspirant must walk the razor's edge before he can hope to reach the immortal abode of surrender.

Speaking mere words like *Aham Brahmasmi*, 'I am Brahman', or *Shivoham*, 'I am Shiva', cannot be the definition of surrender. Many aspirants take up the path of self-realization, thinking they will earn respect and honour for themselves, feigning siddhis that they do not possess, hoping to attract flocks of disciples to pamper their ego. The truth of the matter is that no one wants to discipline themselves and do rigid and systematic sadhana, as it is difficult, so they content themselves with gossiping and meaningless, dry discourses and discussions. A long, grey beard, a kamandalu, an orange robe and a shaved head cannot make one a realized being.

An aspirant who treads the path of samarpan must equip himself with the four means: *viveka*, discrimination, *vairagya*, dispassion, *shadsampat*, six virtues, and *mumukshutva*, desire for liberation. Not an iota of spiritual progress is ever possible unless one is endowed with these fourfold essential qualities. These four spiritual requisites are as old as the Vedas. Every religion prescribes them for the sincere aspirant; only the terms or names differ.

1. Viveka

Viveka is discrimination between real and unreal, *sat* and *asat*, permanent and impermanent, *nitya* and *anitya*, self and non-self, *Atma* and *anatma*. Viveka dawns due to the grace of God, which comes only when one has done incessant, selfless service over countless births with the feeling of *Ishwara arpana*, surrender to the Divine Self. The door of the higher mind is flung open with the awakening of discrimination. An unchanging, permanent principle co-exists amidst the ever-changing phenomena of the universe and the fleeting movements and oscillations of the mind.

The five *koshas* or sheaths of individual existence are floating in the universal consciousness, like straw on water. The five changing koshas are mixed up with the eternal Atman or Supreme Self. This physical body undergoes many stages: infancy, childhood, adolescence, youth, middle age and old age. But there is an unchanging background for this ever-changing body and mind, like the screen in a cinema, which manifests various forms and figures. The witness or silent spectator of these changes in the body and mind is permanent and unchanging, like the all-pervading *akasha*, space. It pervades, permeates and penetrates all these changing forms, like the thread on a garland of flowers.

The eternal essence or Atman is present everywhere and in everything, but it dwells in the chambers of the heart. It is the soul of the tree, stone, flower, goat, dog, cat, man, saint or devata. It is the common property of all, whether saint or sinner, king or peasant, beggar or baron, scavenger or cobbler. It is the very source of life and thought. The aspirant should learn to discriminate between the eternal and unchanging substratum of all objects and the ever-changing names and forms. He should seriously engage himself at all times in separating the eternal, unchanging Self from the changing, impermanent self; from the passions, emotions, feelings, thoughts and sentiments of the oscillating mind.

The aspirant should distinguish between the mind and the witness who moves and illumines the mind; between ordinary sensation, feelings and sentiments, and perfect awareness of pure consciousness, which remains unaffected and unattached, between personality and individuality. He must also separate himself from the adventitious, false superimpositions of the body, namely position, rank, vocation, birth, caste, stage and order. These are all accidental appendages of the false personality. He must totally transcend the ego, the sense of individuality. The world of the ego is in the clutches of Maya, who is charming. The beauty in the flower, the feminine form and the magnificent Himalayas will all turn to dust. Such beauty is only a reflection of that unchanging Self within, the infinite, undecaying beauty of beauties.

The aspirant should also separate himself from the six waves in the ocean of samsara, namely, birth and death, hunger and thirst, exhilaration and grief. Birth and death relate to the physical body, hunger and thirst to the pranic body, and exhilaration and grief to the mind. The Atman, which is subtle like the all-pervading ether, is unattached, *asanga,* and untouched by the six waves. The aspirant should also separate himself from the *indriyas* or senses. He should not identify himself with the functions of the senses. He should stand as a spectator, as a witness of the activities of the mind, prana and senses. The senses and the mind are like pieces of iron in contact with a magnet. They function by borrowing light and power from the source, the eternal Atman.

Meditation on the following verse from the *Bhagavad Gita* and the special formula of Sri Shankaracharya will help in developing viveka and separating oneself from the illusory vehicles of body, prana, senses and mind. The formula of Sri Shankaracharya is: *Brahma Satyam Jagat Mithya; Jiva Brahmaiva Naparah* – 'Brahman (the eternal) is Truth; this world is unreal; the embodied soul is identical to Brahman.' The *Bhagavad Gita* (2:16) says: "The unreal has no being; the real never ceases to be. The truth about both has been perceived by the seers of the Truth or Essence." Reflection on this verse will infuse viveka.

The ordinary man of the world identifies himself with the perishable body, impermanent objects, wife, child, business and property, and hence becomes attached to external names and forms. He develops 'my-ness' and delusion, love and hatred, pride in caste and position. He thinks: "I am a Brahmin. I am a rich man. I am a king. I am a genius. I am very powerful and important. My wife comes from a respected family; she is a university graduate. I am a member of the Legislative Assembly." He brags of his false status, possessions and intellectual attainments, and thus is caught up in the ever-revolving wheel of birth and death. He is born again and again into the world of delusion and undergoes various sorts of miseries, troubles, sorrows and pains, all on account of non-discrimination.

Viveka gives inner strength and mental peace. A viveki has no troubles because he is always alert and never gets entangled in anything. He is far-sighted and knows the true value of the objects of this universe. He is fully aware of the worthlessness of worldly toys and nothing can tempt him. Maya cannot approach him. Association with mahatmas and the study of spiritual literature infuses the mind with such viveka. The aspirant should be firmly established in viveka and develop it to the maximum degree. True viveka is not an ephemeral or occasional mood; it is a constant awareness that will not fail, even in the midst of a crisis. Viveka must become part and parcel of one's nature. It should be exercised at all times, without any effort. In the beginning, the feeling of viveka may come and go, so the aspirant should live in the company of sages for a long time, until viveka burns in him like a large, steady flame. When viveka is developed, all the other qualities will come by themselves.

2. Vairagya

Vairagya is the detachment and dispassion born of viveka, which is enduring and everlasting, and will not fail the aspirant at any time. Vairagya is purely a mental state. A person who lives amidst riches and luxuries may be a greater vairagi than the sadhu who lives in a cave. Raja Janaka and Queen Chudali were absolutely dispassionate while ruling their kingdoms, whereas Raja Sikhidhwaja, though he lived in a forest with only a *kaupeen*, loin cloth, and a *kamandalu*, water pot, had intense attachment to the body.

Vairagya does not mean abandoning the social duties and responsibilities of life. It does not mean living in the solitary caves of the Himalayas or in a cremation ground. It does not mean wearing matted hair and carrying a kamandalu. It does not mean shaving one's head and throwing off one's clothes. Vairagya is mental detachment from all the connections of the world. A man may remain in the world and discharge all the duties of his order and stage of life with detachment. He may be a householder, living with family and children, but at the same time have perfect mental detachment from everything. The person who has perfect mental detachment while remaining in the world is a hero, because he has to face innumerable temptations at every moment.

Wherever a man goes, he carries his fickle, restless mind, his *vasanas* and *samskaras*, desires and impressions, with him. Even in solitude, he is still engaged in thinking of worldly objects, in building castles in the air., so even the solitary cave becomes a big city for him. However, when the mind remains quiet and free from attachments, one can be a perfect vairagi even while living in a mansion in the busiest part of a city. Such a mansion will be converted as though into a deserted forest. Where a person lives and what he wears has nothing to do with vairagya.

The two currents of the mind, attraction and repulsion, constitute the illusory world of *samsara*. The mind becomes intensely attached to those objects from which it derives pleasure. Whenever there is a sensation of pleasure, the mind becomes glued to that object. Such attachment always leads to bondage and pain. Attraction and repulsion, pleasure and pain, co-exist. A worldly person is a slave to these two mighty currents and is tossed between them like a piece of straw, smiling in pleasure and weeping in pain.

A dispassionate person has a different training and experience altogether. He is a past master in the art of separating himself from impermanent, perishable objects. He has absolutely no attraction to them and constantly dwells in the eternal. He identifies himself with the witnessing consciousness that is present in both pleasure and pain. He stands adamantine as a peak amidst a turbulent storm, a spectator of this wonderful world-show. He is not at all affected by pleasant or painful experiences. He learns valuable lessons from every experience in life. He is not afraid of facing life because he knows there is wisdom to gain from every experience.

The aspirant can develop mental detachment from pleasure and pain, attraction and repulsion, even while living in the world. He should not cling to or be carried away by the pleasant experiences of life and should not be afraid of painful or unpleasant experiences. He should remain as a silent spectator, a witness, to every experience in life. By practising in this way, eventually he will develop an unruffled and poised mind. A dispassionate person is the happiest, richest and most powerful person in the world.

Every aspirant should study the scriptures that discuss vairagya. This will induce dispassion in the mind and inspire the desire to apply it in daily life. The remembrance of death and the pain of the world will also help to a considerable extent. There are monks who keep a human skull to remind them of the impermanent and perishable nature of life. A philosopher kept the skull of a lady he had once been intimate with and began to speak thus: "O skull! Sometime back you tempted me with your shiny skin, lotus eyes, honeyed lips and rosy cheeks. Now where are your charms?" He thus convinced himself of the impermanent nature of the body and mind and was able to live in the state of vairagya.

The desire for sensual enjoyment is deeply-rooted in the minds of all. The rajasic mind cannot remain even for a single moment without thoughts of enjoyment. Modern civilization is another name for sensual enjoyment. Bars, restaurants, holiday resorts and the enormous range of entertainments intensify sensual enjoyment. People invent new dishes, new drinks and new ingredients to satisfy the palate. Fashion in dress, hair styles and cosmetics are constantly changing. Even the aspirant wishes to discover intense and lasting enjoyments by means of yogic practice; these are the subtle temptations. The sincere aspirant will resolutely turn away from all forms of entertainment and treat them as vomited matter, offal or poison.

3. Shadsampat

Shadsampat are the six virtues, consisting of *sama*, mental tranquillity, *dama*, sense control, *uparati*, sense withdrawal, *titiksha*, endurance, *shraddha*, faith, and *samadhana*, mental balance. These six are taken as one, because they are all calculated to bring about mental control and discipline, and ultimately surrender to the Absolute.

Sama: Sama is serenity or tranquillity of mind that is brought about by eradication of the *vasanas*, subtle desires, and modifications of the mind. The mind is kept within the chamber of the heart and not allowed to move outside with the sensual objects. In this way the mind becomes fixed on the source. Serenity of mind is most important for spiritual aspirants and must become part of their being before samarpan can be realized. The mind is the commander of the ten senses: the five organs of perception and the five organs of action. Control of the senses cannot be perfected unless the mind is managed correctly. No sense can work independently without the cooperation of the mind. When sama is established, dama, or control of the senses, comes by itself.

Dama: Dama is mental control of the senses, not blunting or deadening the senses by foolish austerities. If the mind is managed, what can the sensory organs do? The senses should be consecrated to the lotus feet of the Lord for His service. The ten senses are ten powers and, if used correctly, they are beneficial when serving the guru and other saints. The tongue can repeat the guru stotras; the ears can hear the shrutis and other religious scriptures. What is required is judicious management of the senses. They should not be allowed to run riot into sensual grooves. If the senses are properly disciplined and kept under control, they become useful servants. Daily observance of mouna, regulation of the diet and moderation of sexual activities are of great help in controlling the senses. One who understands this and is able to manage the mind and senses will reach the end of this journey, whence he is not born again in the round of birth and death.

Uparati: Uparati is the turning away of the mind from objects of sensual desire and enjoyment. This state of mind comes naturally when one has practised viveka, vairagya, sama and dama. Sri Shankaracharya defines uparati in *Viveka Chudamani* as follows: "The best uparati or sense withdrawal consists of the mind ceasing to act by means of external objects." Uparati is the state of mind which is always engaged inwardly, without being diverted.

Titiksha: Titiksha is the power of endurance. A wise person never grumbles because he understands the divine plan. He tries to fix the mind in the permanent, unchanging, witnessing consciousness within himself, which is beyond all the pairs of opposites, and then watches the movement and the phenomena of this universe with an unruffled mind. Some take titiksha as the end, but it is only the means. A little practice will serve the purpose. The aspirant should patiently bear the pairs of opposites, such as heat and cold, pleasure and pain.

In *Viveka Chudamani* Sri Shankaracharya defines titiksha as: "Forbearance, bearing of all afflictions without caring to redress them; at the same time being free from anxiety or lamentation on their score." In the *Bhagavad Gita* (2:14–15), Lord Krishna advises Arjuna: "The contact of the senses with the objects which cause sensations of heat and cold, pleasure and pain, have a beginning and an end; they are impermanent. Endure them bravely, O Arjuna. The firm man whom these afflict not, who is balanced in pleasure and pain, is fit to attain immortality."

Everything appears as a play of the Divine to the practitioner of titiksha. He sees intelligence in every inch of creation. He has a very comprehensive understanding of the laws of nature and the pairs of opposites. He understands the reason for the existence of pain, snakes, scorpions, tigers, etc. This is true titiksha, based on knowledge and experience of life, not merely a mental concept. This practitioner can endure any kind of difficulty or catastrophe and is not shaken by shocking news or heavy sorrow.

Shraddha: Shraddha is faith. Even the greatest philosopher has faith as his stronghold. No intellectual theory can be proved if it is not supported by faith. The whole world stands on faith and is guided by faith. All religions are rooted in faith. One cannot prove the existence of God if he has no faith in God. Faith is not the voice of the mind, which deludes, but the voice of the soul that uplifts and takes one to the goal. The aspirant should cling fast to faith in divine possibilities and constantly aspire to live in the Divine.

Faith is guided by the impressions of actions done in previous births. One's present faith is nearer or farther from the truth in accordance with the advancement one has made in spiritual evolution. Faith without understanding is blind faith, which should be turned to rational faith through understanding. Bhakti is the development of faith, and jnana is the development of bhakti. Faith leads to the ultimate experience. Whatever a person strongly believes in, he experiences and becomes that.

The whole world is a product of faith and imagination. Without faith in the world, the world does not exist. Without faith in sensual objects, they will not give pleasure. Without faith in God, one can never reach surrender and perfection. Faith is the fundamental necessity for all spiritual practice. Aspiration is the development of faith; it is one step ahead of faith. The flame of faith becomes the conflagration of spiritual aspiration. The devotee longs to have union with the Beloved. He has no sleep, no rest. He always contemplates how to attain the object of his love. He prays and sings to his Lord, and a type of divine madness overtakes him. He completely loses his personality in the aspiration for attaining God. This is the kind of faith required for samarpan.

An aspirant perceives distance, distinction and separation from God inasmuch as he depends on the external world and believes and experiences its necessity. However, with faith in God as his own inner essence, the world will eventually fall away and the devotee will experience nearness, identification and the feeling of non-separation from God. This experience is possible only through faith and the feeling that all beings are His manifestation.

Samadhana: Samadhana refers to mental balance. This is the fruit of the practice of sama, dama, uparati, titiksha and shraddha. Samadhana is fixing the mind on the Atman and not allowing it to run towards objects and have its own way. It is self-settledness. In *Atma Anatma Viveka,* Sri Shankaracharya defines samadhana as follows: "The mind engaged in worship or contemplation wanders to any worldly object or desire and, finding it worthless, returns to the object of contemplation. Such returning is called samadhana." In this state the mind is free from anxiety amidst pain and indifferent amidst pleasure. There is stability of mind and mental peace.

The aspirant who has developed samadhana lives without attachment. He neither likes nor dislikes and so has great strength of mind and unruffled supreme peace. Some aspirants have peace of mind when they live in seclusion, where there are no distracting elements or factors, but when they come to a city and mix with people, they complain of great distractions, tossing of the mind, or *vikshepa*, and are completely upset. They cannot do any meditation in a crowded place. This is a weakness, not the achievement of samadhana. There is no balance of mind or equanimity in such people.

Only when the mind remains as balanced on the battlefield of confusing circumstances as it is in a secluded Himalayan cave is samadhana fully established. In the *Bhagavad Gita* (2:48), Lord Krishna says: "Perform all actions, O Arjuna, dwelling in union with the Divine, renouncing attachment and with the mind balanced in success and failure." This is samadhana. Again Lord Krishna says (2:64): "The disciplined mind, moving among objects with the senses under restraint and free from attraction and repulsion, attains peace." This is also samadhana.

4. Mumukshutva

Mumukshutva is intense desire for liberation, or deliverance from the wheel of birth and death with its concomitant evils of old age, disease, delusion and sorrow. If one is equipped with the previous three qualifications of viveka, vairagya and shadsampat, mumukshutva will come by itself. The mind moves towards its source of its own accord, because it has lost its hold on external objects and has no resting place in the objective universe.

Purification of the mind and mental discipline form the foundation of yoga. When these are perfected, the longing for surrender dawns by itself. If burning mumukshutva is coupled with burning vairagya, surrender will come within the twinkling of an eye. Generally, the vast majority of people have a dull type of vairagya and mumukshutva, so they do not succeed in their attempts. In the absence of burning mumukshutva, one must practise the other three: viveka, vairagya and shadsampat, vigorously until he acquires intense longing for attaining divine communion.

Eventually, all the four requisites should be mastered to the maximum degree. Proficiency in one requisite alone will not make one ready. There is a definite significance in the sequence of the four requisites. The aspirant who is endowed with these four should receive satsang from a *Brahmanishta* guru, one established in direct knowledge of Brahman, and then reflect and meditate on the inner Self. He will become fit for the highest sadhana. The aspirant in possession of these four jewels is a blessed divinity on this earth, and will attain absolute surrender.

6
Transcendence of Desire

Samarpan is the very essence of devotional love. The ultimate form of love is surrender. Divine love has no element of desire in it. All worldly desires disappear the moment bhakti dawns. The devotee does not expect any reward from God. He loves God for love's sake, not for his own gain. Absolute surrender cannot co-exist with desire of any kind, not even the desire for liberation. The devotee wants God and His service alone. He does not accept any reward or boon, even when offered the five forms of liberation, because desire obstructs the growth of devotion. When mundane desires are renounced, devotion to the Lord increases in intensity.

Samarpan is not practised for any selfish purpose whatsoever. The devotee does not want prosperity, power or even release from pain and suffering. The basis of unconditional love, supreme love and divine love is complete self-surrender. The renunciation of worldly activities and duties does not mean abandonment of such activities themselves, but the annihilation of craving, egoism, selfishness and attachment to results. Activities that maintain life cannot be stopped, but they can be consecrated or dedicated to the Lord by complete surrender.

As Lord Krishna tells Arjuna in the *Bhagavad Gita* (3:4–5, 9): "Not by merely abstaining from work can one achieve freedom from reaction, nor by renunciation alone can one attain perfection . . . Everyone is forced to act helplessly by the *gunas* or qualities born of Nature. No one can refrain from action, even for a moment . . . Work must be performed with an attitude of surrender to God, otherwise work causes bondage in this material world. Therefore, O son of Kunti, perform your prescribed duties for His satisfaction, and you will always remain free from bondage."

For the realized devotee the distinction between sacred and secular duty vanishes. Every work is a sacred offering unto the Lord. Every work is an expression of this love for God. A worldly-minded person cannot work without the expectation of fruits. He is caught up in the never-ending wheel of samsara. The rishis, seers, and the Vedas, therefore, advise that all works should be consecrated to the Lord and performed without any expectation of fruits. Then the heart is purified and bhakti develops. That is why in the *Bhagavad Gita* (9:27) Lord Krishna advises Arjuna: "Whatever you do, whatever you eat, whatever you offer in sacrifice, whatever you give, whatever austerities you perform, do it as an offering to Me."

Maharishi Patanjali also says in the *Yoga Sutras* (1:23) that complete surrender of one's will to the Lord leads to *samadhi*, or union with Him. Success is rapid in attaining samadhi by surrendering the fruits of work as offerings at the feet of the Lord. *Ishwara pranidhana*, surrender to God, is an important aspect of Patanjali's raja yoga.

Slay the ego

Egoism, ambition and subtle desires are obstacles in the way of self surrender. The subtle hidden desires will try to come to the surface of the mind. Desire which is suppressed for some time will again manifest with redoubled force if the aspirant is not careful, if there is some waning force in his detachment and sadhana, and if he mixes with worldly-minded people. Generally, the aspirant, consciously or unconsciously, wittingly or unwittingly, retains some desires for his gratification. He does not wish to part completely with his desires. Therefore, self-surrender is not perfect and unreserved, and the grace of God does not descend. There is no possibility of divine grace if there is even an atom of desire or egoism.

The Lord becomes the slave of a bhakta only when the bhakta has made absolute and ungrudging self-surrender. He is very cruel and puts His devotee to severe tests and trials. All desires, selfishness, likes and dislikes, vanity and fear of death hang on egoism. The pivot upon which all of these are centred is egoism. Kill egoism, then surrender becomes complete. Even if there is a tinge of egoism, the Lord will not reveal Himself. Surrender everything to the Lord. Do every action as an offering unto Him. Single-mindedness is an important factor in devotion. When you surrender your mind, ego and body to the Lord, you will realize your oneness with Him.

A devotee realizes that the Lord alone is acting through him, that God alone has given him intelligence and opportunities, and he does not take any credit for himself. He attributes everything to God's grace. A worldly person forgets about God and allows his ego to assert itself at every step. The real barrier to complete surrender is ego. Slay it! It is the enemy of devotion and peace. Be indifferent to its persuasions and promptings. Place it as an offering at the lotus feet of the Lord. This is the real flower that can be offered to Him. A mother always thinks of her child. A passionate husband always thinks of his wife. A greedy man always thinks of his money. Even so the devotee will always entertain God in his heart.

Cultivate detachment
Single-minded devotion can only manifest by the constant and protracted practice of discrimination and detachment. Whenever the wavering and unsteady mind runs out, curb it, draw it in and fix it again and again at the feet of the Lord. It takes some time for the mind to establish new habits, as it is naturally prone to love of comfort and ease, gluttony, laziness, gossiping, worldly talk and sight-seeing. It should gradually

be tamed, trained and disciplined by suitable methods. Patience, perseverance, attention, faith, strong will, fortitude and power of endurance are required. These virtues need to be cultivated through *satsang*, association with the wise, and the practice of *yama* and *niyama*, personal and ethical restraints.

An aspirant must cherish perfect detachment towards sensual enjoyment and objects, and destroy any infatuation for these. Infatuated love for the body, children, father, mother, wife or husband is completely different to a devotee's absolute love of God. Attachment to the body is deep-rooted. Thoughts of the body, food, wife and children alone can make you forget God. In the *Bhagavad Gita* (13:9–10), Lord Krishna advises Arjuna: "Cultivate freedom from attachment and identification with children, wife or husband, home and the rest; constant even-mindedness amidst pleasant and unpleasant events; detachment from worldly-minded people, and constant and unswerving devotion to Me."

An attitude of detachment towards sensual enjoyments and objects destroys all sorts of infatuations and desires. Attachment is death; detachment is eternal life. One who is detached from the world experiences the worldly drama as a witness and passes beyond grief. Detachment is neither inaction nor foolish austerities; rather it is upholding a mental attitude in the course of daily action. Worldly people attach importance to external show only and this is their mistake. A person may have nothing, yet his mind may be full of desires. A renunciate may be attached to his loin cloth or begging bowl although he lives alone in a forest, whereas a king may remain perfectly detached although he lives amidst luxuries and opulence.

Depend upon God alone

The state of surrender may be disturbed by various influences in daily life. When desires and cravings trouble the devotee, he should not seek the help of agents other than those employed in the cultivation of devotion, such as listening to stories about the Lord, singing His name, selfless service, and so on. The devotee knows no one other than his beloved Lord. The Lord is all in all, the sole refuge for him. He lives for the Lord and works for Him alone. Thus the Lord becomes his sole support, his only strength and his only object of faith. His eyes are fixed on his beloved Lord alone and he sees nothing else besides his Lord. His very existence is held in the hands of his Lord. Why then should he to seek the shelter of any other person?

All the objects of this world are perishable. Nothing other than God can protect one from the troubles of this world. Therefore, the devotee abandons attachment to everything in this world and depends upon God and God alone, who is eternal, omnipotent and all merciful. Through detachment and discrimination, all cravings for pleasure should be destroyed. Then the mind should be turned towards God by constant, steady practice of mantra japa. The struggle for a beginner to direct his mental energy towards God is hard, whereas it is easy to direct the same mental energy towards sensual objects.

The mind naturally runs towards external objects without the least exertion. In the *Bhagavad Gita* (8:8), Lord Krishna says: "One who meditates on Me as the Supreme Lord, his mind constantly engaged in remembering Me, without deviating from the path, is sure to reach Me." Further Lord Krishna states (12:8–9): "Fix your mind on Me only and engage your intellect in Me, then you will live in Me always, without a doubt . . . If you are unable to fix your mind steadily on Me, then by the yoga of constant practice develop a desire to attain Me, O Arjuna."

The *Bhagavad Gita*, *Srimad Bhagavatam* and all the sacred scriptures are guides to the path of surrender. The guru interprets the sacred scriptures and guides the devotee. All works which help to cultivate devotion must be regularly practised. There must be active cooperation with the divine plan. The aspirant must have faith in the existence of God if he is to perform sacrifice, penance and charity. All actions must be done for His sake; only then are they beneficial and enduring. A devotee does not do any action which is not pleasing to God, which does not help in the growth of devotion, which goes against the will of his Lord.

Prahlada renounced his atheistic father; Vibhishana, his demonic brother; Bharata, his cruel mother; Bali, his preceptor; the gopis of Vraj, their husbands. But they all contributed to the welfare of the world and are regarded as great devotees of the Lord. The devotee does all those actions which are pleasing to the Lord until he attains God-realization. He abandons activities prohibited by the scriptures, such as theft, adultery, meat-eating and liquor. He abandons all selfish actions. The devotee does obligatory and incidental duties in strict conformity with the procedures laid down in the Vedas without any expectation of the fruits. In the *Bhagavad Gita* (12:10) Lord Krishna says: "If you are unable to practise the principles of yoga, then just try to work for Me, because even by doing actions for My sake, you will attain perfection."

Three kinds of austerities

The performance of rituals purifies the heart and prepares the ego for the development of devotion and surrender. These actions should be performed without attachment and expectation of fruit as enjoined by the scriptures, with the firm belief that sacrifice is duty; it is pure action. Lord Krishna says in the *Bhagavad Gita* (18:5): "Acts of sacrifice, charity and penance are not to be given up; they must be performed. Indeed, sacrifice, charity and penance purify even the great souls." The three kinds of austerities: physical, verbal and mental, prescribed in the seventeenth chapter of the *Bhagavad Gita* purify the heart. They are as follows:

1. Physical – devotion in action

> Austerities of the body consist of worship of the Supreme Lord, the twice-born, the spiritual master and the wise, purity, simplicity, celibacy and non-violence. (17:14)

Austerities, daily worship and giving gifts on special occasions should not be neglected. Abundant information on these practices is detailed in the Hindu texts *Code of Manu* and *Yajnavalkya Smriti*. If it is difficult to consult the scriptures, the guidance of *pandits* and *acharyas*, scholars and teachers, may be sought. Observance of these rituals helps to purify the body.

2. Verbal – devotion in speech

> Austerity of speech consists of recitation of the scriptures and speaking words that are truthful, straightforward, beneficial and not agitating to others. (17:15)

Talking about the Lord's glory and greatness, and a fondness for spiritual discussion are the signs of devotion. *Katha* is narration, *patha* is reading stories, *sankirtan* is collective chanting with musical instruments, *Hari kathas* are discourses on spiritual topics, *bhajan* is singing hymns. Hearing and repeating the stories of the Lord removes impurities of speech and ultimately leads to God-realization. Stories of the incarnations of God are most elevating, inspiring and soul-stirring, and they instil devotion in the hearts of listeners. Lord Krishna says in the *Bhagavad Gita* (10:9): "My pure devotees derive great satisfaction and bliss from always conversing about Me and thus enlightening one another."

3. Mental – devotion in mind

> Mental austerity consists of serenity, good-heartedness, gentleness, silence, self-control and purity of nature. (17:16)

Being established in calmness, free from depression and confusion, is serenity. Thinking in a kind way towards all is gentleness. Remaining in a state of mental equilibrium is silence. Allowing only pure and noble thoughts to arise in the mind is self-control. One who has attained mastery over the mind never utters unwanted words or performs undesirable actions.

This threefold austerity performed with utmost faith, without desire for the fruits, is said to be pure. Without purification of body, speech and mind, there is no hope of cultivating devotion and surrender in the heart. There cannot be real surrender unless there is purity and self-control in thought, word and deed. It is necessary to worship God and sing His praises. However, pooja, narrations, etc. are all inferior to that kind of devotion in which the ego is totally surrendered. In pooja and narrations, the devotee does not need to surrender his ego. In self-surrender there is effacement of the ego. Any selfless work performed without egoism, with the attitude of self surrender, has a real place in devotional or spiritual life. It is a real offering to the Lord.

Importance of scriptural observance

There should be strict adherence to the injunctions of the *shastras* or scriptures until a firm conviction in God is attained and until profound devotion is fully established. Actions enjoined by the scriptures should be diligently performed until that state of absolute forgetfulness of external existence is reached. Even after firm establishment in divine resolve, the scriptures must be respected. The scriptures are the words of God; they are the guiding lights for aspirants. Swerving even an inch from the path chalked out by the shastras will bring about a downfall for the devotee. Some deluded aspirants foolishly imagine that they have attained perfection and are above the laws of the scriptures, so they cease to observe them and suffer hopeless downfalls.

An aspirant must first have intellectual conviction and then firmness in living up to the ideal. He must practise and live up to the principles which he knows by conviction are essential for his happiness, spiritual evolution and God-realization. The personal examples of fellow devotees, who are sure and steady in their daily observances, exercise a tremendous influence over others. Realized people follow the scriptures in their actual life and thus set examples for the ordinary person, who needs constant guidance in his life. When one is established in *dharma*, righteousness, one is eligible to protect the shastras. By living up to the ideals of these texts, one protects their teachings. In the *Bhagavad Gita* (16:24), Lord Krishna says: "Let the scriptures be the authority in determining what ought to be done and ought not to be done. Knowing these rules and regulations, one should act here in this world accordingly and be elevated gradually."

If the devotee who has made some spiritual progress is not careful and does not observe the rules of the scriptures, he may easily relapse into past habits. Just as a young plant is fully protected in the beginning, so also a neophyte on the path of devotion should be well protected. If he mixes with worldly-minded people, he will lose his faith in God quickly. He must always be in the company of sadhus, mahatmas and bhaktas. Their company is an iron fortress for him. If the injunctions of the shastras are followed rigidly, nothing can shake one's conviction. Just as a nail is driven deep into a plank by frequent hammering, so also the spiritual impressions and convictions become deep by strictly observing the sacred laws of the scriptures.

If the mind of an aspirant follows the injunctions of the shastras, he will not suffer uneasiness and will evolve quickly. He will feel that he is on the right path and is progressing spiritually. He will feel the nearness of God and have peace of mind. He will be cheerful, fearless and satisfied. One who deliberately violates the rules of good conduct prescribed by the scriptures will surely fall and return to his previous state of worldliness and ignorance. Lord Krishna says in the *Bhagavad Gita* (16:23): "One who discards scriptural injunctions and acts according to his own whims attains neither perfection nor happiness, nor the Supreme Goal."

The scriptures are infallible. They are revelations which have been traditionally handed down from the rishis and seers to their disciples in succession. The realized sages prune away the superfluities and excrescences when the times necessitate readjustments. This remoulding does not change the essence of the scriptures; rather it allows the concepts to continue through the passage of time and remain relevant to man's quest for the supreme attainment. The Vedas have come from the mouth of God. The scriptures and the spiritual teachers will thus always be there to guide people in the path of truth and righteousness. The concepts in the Vedas are eternal, although the books may not be.

Maya is very powerful
Mysterious is the power of infatuation and desire. That is why Lord Krishna says in the *Bhagavad Gita* (2:60–61): "The senses are so turbulent, O Arjuna, that they forcibly carry away the mind even of a wise man who is striving to control them. One who restrains the senses, keeping them under control and fixes his consciousness upon Me is known as a man of steady wisdom." The sadhaka must be very careful. A beginner is unable to resist temptations and falls prey to their influence quite readily, so he should not test his spiritual strength at the very outset when he has made only a little progress. His senses may revolt and his mind may become a victim of passions.

Those who are put to tests by their guru can easily fail, even in the higher stages of devotion. Rishi Vishwamitra, the great tapasvi, fell under the influence of a celestial nymph. Similarly, Lord Buddha had to face the power of maya. This world is full of temptations. There is the possibility of downfall at every moment. Physical control alone will not suffice; there must also be mental stability. The *Bhagavad Gita* states (3:6): "One who restrains the senses of action, but whose mind dwells on sense objects, deludes himself and is called a hypocrite."

Some young sadhakas do sadhana for four or five years in the Himalayan caves, see some dazzling lights during meditation, hear some *anahata*, 'unstruck', sounds in the ears and think they are realized souls. They re-enter the world to preach and mix freely with householders. They fail rapidly in their spiritual endeavour. What is gained by twelve years of rigid sadhana can be easily lost in twelve seconds if one mixes promiscuously with householders and does not take proper precautions. The sadhaka should remain in sadhana until he becomes fully established in the highest state of consciousness. He should adhere to the injunctions of the spiritual disciplines until supreme devotion has transformed his existence. Observances will then drop away by themselves when one is firmly established in the highest devotion.

All worldly duties, such as one's occupation in life, maintaining the family and environment etc., should also be carefully and scrupulously performed along with spiritual duties, according to the injunctions of the scriptures. It must also be remembered that one cannot serve God and humanity without good health. Therefore, eating and drinking properly to nourish the body must continue as long as one lives. Preservation of health is the way to success in sadhana, rather than merely existing on a starvation diet. A time will come when the devotee is fully established in supreme devotion and surrender to God. Then all activities, spiritual as well as mundane, will drop away by themselves, and the devotee will be able to safely leave the scriptural as well as customary injunctions.

Give up desire

The feeling of 'mineness' grows through constant association with sensual objects. It is very difficult to eradicate this feeling. Attachment assumes various subtle forms, even in the most devoted aspirants. It lingers even in the minds of great men. It comes in the name of patriotism, institution, organization, religion, service for humanity, etc. One must cut all attachments ruthlessly, only then will absolute surrender develop. In the *Bhagavad Gita* (2:71–72), Lord Krishna says: "When a man abandons all desires, and is without the sense of 'I' and 'mine', his mind thus purified finds satisfaction in the Self alone. Then he attains Moksha or eternal peace, and oneness with the eternal Brahman."

A devotee who has surrendered everything will be able to rise above all earthly desires, his heart being full of supreme peace. He does not desire anything, being conscious of the illusory and unreal nature of worldly objects, and no longer takes any interest in them. His thirst for sensual pleasure has been quenched forever by the attainment of God-realization. His heart is full, so kingdom, wealth and power have no attraction for him. Desires arise from a sense of imperfection or limitation and manifest because of ignorance, *avidya*, imperfection and lack of bliss. The feeling of imperfection arises only when a person identifies with something outside of himself, other than himself. When one receives the darshan of God, all desires are burnt up. When the boy Dhruva had darshan of Lord Hari, the desire that prompted him to worship the Lord disappeared. Devotion is a fire, like the fire of wisdom, that burns up all mundane desires. When a devotee attains God-realization, he is not conscious of anything other than God. Therefore, a devotee becomes absolutely desireless.

Subtle desire, *vasana*, draws a person outside towards external objects. Ignorance has two forces, the veiling power that screens one from his real essence, and the power of distraction that makes the mind and senses outgoing. Restlessness of mind is due to desire and distraction. Ignorance clouds the understanding, produces intoxication, destroys the intellect and makes the intellect perverted, stony and barren. Therefore, a person always thinks that he can find pleasure in external objects. He mistakes his body, children and wife for the Atma, and perceives the unreal world as real.

When lust manifests, the intellect becomes blind. The most intelligent person vainly searches for happiness in outside, perishable objects. The idea of meditating on God never strikes him. He does not believe in devotion, concentration and meditation. He cannot imagine a pure, unalloyed happiness that is independent of external objects, although he enjoys the bliss of the Self every night during deep sleep. He thinks: "If I have a son, if I have a new car, I will be happy." This is due to the force of ignorance. The sincere devotee must give up this unquenchable thirst for sensual pleasure, relationships, money and worldly prosperity, which is the greatest obstacle in the path of devotion, and turn the mind towards God. Here is an inexhaustible and imperishable spiritual wealth that no thief can rob, a divine bliss that is not mixed with fear or pain.

Desire is an enemy of peace and devotion. Without renunciation of desire, surrender can never be cultivated in the heart. Attachment to sensual enjoyment is the greatest obstacle in developing devotion and surrender. Energy leaks out and no improvement is seen in spiritual sadhana. The devotee always complains: "I have not realized anything on the path of devotion. My mind remains in the same state. It always wanders about wildly in sensual grooves." Desire is very powerful and assumes various subtle forms. Desire is maya's weapon to hurl down the *jivas*, individual souls, into the mire of worldly infatuation. There is no end to desires; they are unconquerable unless one takes to the path of selfless service. Enjoyment does not bring satisfaction of a desire. Desire is strengthened by enjoyment, just as fire is increased by pouring ghee on it.

Self-restraint

For this reason Lord Krishna says in the *Bhagavad Gita* (3:37–41, 43): "It is only desire, born of contact with the material mode of rajas, and later transformed into anger, which is the all-devouring, sinful enemy in this world. As fire is enveloped by smoke, as a mirror by dust, or the embryo by the womb, the living entity is similarly covered by different degrees of desire. Thus the pure consciousness becomes enveloped by its eternal enemy in the form of desire, which is never satisfied and burns like fire. The senses, mind and intellect are the seats of desire; through these it veils wisdom and deludes the mind. Therefore, O Arjuna, curb this desire in the very beginning by regulating the senses, and slay this destroyer of knowledge and self-realization . . . Knowing oneself to be superior to the intellect and restraining the self by the Self, O mighty-armed Arjuna, steady the mind by constant spiritual effort and thus conquer the insatiable enemy known as desire."

Attachment should be annihilated first and then the longing will die by itself. Eventually preference also will be destroyed. When the attraction towards external objects ceases, there still remains a thirsting habit for internal objects. This is another dangerous enemy of devotion. When the attraction towards external as well as internal objects ceases without any veil, then one is freed from the habit of desire. This is the strong chain of longing from which the devotee should unshackle himself if he wants to grow in surrender. The thread of sense hankering must be cut off with the sword of discrimination. This is control of desire, *nirodha*. Those who desire salvation alone may follow the path of *samarpan*, absolute surrender, because this path easily cuts asunder the bondages of the world. It attracts God Himself, who becomes the object of one's love and adoration. Final emancipation is very difficult to attain, but in the state of total surrender salvation happens unsolicited. Therefore, one should become a *mumukshu*, seeker of liberation. Do not desire anything other than the Lord. Only then will God choose you. He will lift you up from the mire of this worldly life.

7
Faith, Grace and Divine Will

Samarpan is the last stage of bhakti yoga, where there is absolute faith in and realization of the soul's oneness with God. The self or the ego is surrendered or parted with forever as an offering to the Lord, and the devotee is lost in God-consciousness. He has plunged into the ocean of bliss, taken a bath in the sea of nectar and drunk deeply the essence of immortality. He has become an *apta kama*, a realized sage, for he has attained God, the Divine, and the root of the universe. In this respect, Lord Jesus was able to say: "I and my Father are one."

Intense, unswerving faith is the first requisite in the quest for surrender to God. Faith is the life and strength of a devotee. One who has faith has everything. Faith alone takes one to God. Surrender is attained only according to the measure in which one has faith. One must trust in the Lord with all one's heart and acknowledge Him in all ways. God directs the sincere aspirant on the spiritual path and helps him at every step. He blesses and inspires him and throws light upon the path.

Greatness of faith
Faith is the fundamental key to successful surrender in spiritual life. It is the key to perennial peace and eternal bliss. The power of faith is such that, as Christ put it, even a grain of faith can move a mountain. The one duty of a

devotee is to surrender to Him alone for rest, light and salvation. Lord Jesus said: "Only the one who does the will of my heavenly Father shall enter into the kingdom of heaven." Sincere feelings of dedication and surrender are what take one to God, not verbal humility and devotion. Spiritual effort is not aimed towards public worship, adoration in the streets and beating of drums, but silent sacrifice and intense feeling of union with the One without a second. Christ said: "Blessed are they who hunger and thirst after righteousness, for they shall be filled. Blessed are they who mourn, for they shall be comforted. Blessed are they who are persecuted for the sake of righteousness, for theirs is the kingdom of heaven."

The greatness of the devotee's faith in God is a mighty force that makes itself felt by all, by its very presence. "They are the light of the world; a city that is set on a hill cannot be hidden." Faith is the spiritual essence that constitutes the core of a person in union with the Divine. The sun does not proclaim itself when it rises in the sky, but its very presence makes itself felt by those who have eyes to see and sense to feel.

God does not reveal Himself to the devotee until he has the faith to sacrifice his life for His sake. Self-surrender is only possible for the devotee who has total faith and conviction and is able to leave aside his worldly personality and allow the divine plan to unfold through him. When an aspirant possesses his own mind, his own personal identity and individuality, his will differs from that of the Supreme. He must allow himself to be led by the divine will with the ever increasing conviction that the Supreme Self within is the ocean of compassion and love. The will of one with faith in himself is dependent on the will of the Supreme God.

Faith allows the devotee to reach the realms where reason and intellect have no power. Intellectual groping in the darkness of worldly existence gives way to direct perception of God. He no longer argues, reasons or believes; rather he perceives and senses. His seeing of God, feeling of God and enjoying of God is higher than everything else. Satsang, faith, single-minded devotion to one's ideal, intense love for God, *bhava*, inner feeling, and *prema*, divine love, bring the devotee face to face with God.

Faith is the most important qualification for one wanting to embrace samarpan sadhana. In fact, no spiritual progress is possible without firm faith. From faith comes *nishta*, one-pointed devotion. From devotion comes the ability to live in communion with the Divine and to be self-realized. If the faith is flickering, it may soon die and the aspirant will drift aimlessly hither and thither.

Faith and belief
Faith is not blind belief; it grows out of the wisdom of the heart. Surrender is possible through faith alone because it releases God's power. Have faith that you can surrender yourself and your all to the Lord. Surrender to the Lord totally; keep nothing back, not even a little pride. Say to the Lord: "Give me only what is best for me, because only You know what that is." A life of absolute faith in the Lord will always be successful in the long run. This is not blind faith or belief; it is based on reasoning, evidence and experience. Only such faith can be lasting, perfect and unshakeable.

Superstitious belief in religious traditions or social customs cannot further one's spiritual advancement. The mind will be restless and doubts will surface. Religious followers often force their beliefs upon others in order to convert them and strengthen their numbers. However, the convert finds no real solace in the newly embraced sect and soon embraces another. The devotee with faith in God acquires *nimitta bhava*, the attitude of being an instrument in the hands of God. He develops a subtle reasoning faculty that enables him to be an observer of all the favourable and unfavourable developments in life. He maintains the inner attitude that the Self within him is always a detached witness. The sincere devotee prays to the Lord for increased faith and devotion to bring him closer to God. Faith delivers the devotee into communion with and ultimately total self-surrender to God.

Divine grace

Through self-surrender the devotee experiences the reality of divine grace and the Lord's readiness to help and support him at all times. The divine influence streams into his being and moulds it into a fit medium for divine realization and instrumentality. Surrender and grace are interrelated. Surrender draws down grace, and grace makes the surrender complete. Surrender starts the purification of the heart and grace completes it. Without grace, complete unification is not possible. Grace divinizes one's being so that the constant flow of inspiration can be received and retained. Through divine grace alone, one's whole being is galvanized and rejuvenated.

The sages speak of four types of grace:

1. *Ishwara kripa, the grace of God*: When the flame of aspiration is kindled in the heart of an aspirant, it is said that he has received the grace of God. He has been as if chosen by God to follow the blessed path that will exalt him to divine consciousness.
2. *Atma kripa, the grace of one's own self*: When an aspirant pursues the spiritual path with tenacity and perseverance, it is said that he has received the grace of his own self, as if his innermost self is permitting him to keep his spiritual resolve.
3. *Guru kripa, the grace of the spiritual preceptor*: When an aspirant pursing the spiritual path is able to withstand temptations and overcome obstacles in a miraculous manner, it is said that he has received the grace of his spiritual preceptor. He has become sensitive to his guru's spiritual influence.
4. *Shastra kripa, the grace of the scriptures*: When an aspirant, while studying the scriptures, is able to understand their subtle meanings as if the scriptures are disclosing their secrets to him, it is said that he has received the grace of the scriptures.

These different types of grace are mutually interdependent. In fact, ishwara kripa is the sole reality behind the other types of grace. The sages have emphasized God's grace as the one and only ruling force of the entire existence, and that it is impossible to advance on the spiritual path without grace. The divine plan creates the spiritual path that leads an aspirant towards self-realization. However, all spiritual paths reveal their secrets under the influence of a spiritual guide.

Self-effort versus grace

Vedantins are in favour of self-effort, while bhaktas advocate divine grace. However, bhaktas say that self-effort is necessary initially for self-purification to enable God's grace to manifest. Although self-effort is necessary, the aspirant soon realizes that he can attain nothing without the grace of the Lord.

Some explain that the law of karma is also an aspect of grace. The Lord has given free will to choose between good and evil, and then waits until man turns to Him of his own accord. That is why it may appear that not everyone is saved by the Lord's grace. However, He bestows His grace on all as soon as He sees man's predilection for Him, so the doctrines of free will and of grace can be satisfactorily reconciled.

Others say that grace is only an aspect of karma. Good acts such as devotion and self surrender produce their result, namely, the grace of God, under the law of karma. Self-effort is possible only through divine grace, which comes automatically when the ego is annihilated. When the obstruction to the flow of divine grace is removed, the grace flows freely. In the *Bhagavad Gita* (7:14), Lord Krishna says: "This divine illusion of Mine, made up of the three qualities of Nature, is difficult to cross over; those who have surrendered to Me alone go beyond this illusion." Lord Krishna further says (18:56): "Doing all kinds of actions always, taking refuge in Me, by My grace one attains the eternal, imperishable abode."

The *Kathopanishad* says: "Even a drop of grace is quite sufficient to free oneself from the trammels of this samsara. It is through the grace of the Lord alone that a man can stick to the spiritual path and break all sorts of ties and attachments."

Grace and surrender

The devotee must have faith that divine grace always descends when the time is ripe. If he feels there is a delay in the descent of divine light and grace, he should not give up the struggle. It is very difficult to say when and how divine grace will descend. One should be equipped with the necessary qualifications and make oneself fit for the company of the Divine. If one realizes the Lord's company and willingly surrenders his whole being to the divine teachings, the question of salvation is solved.

In the final chapter of the *Bhagavad Gita* (18:66), Lord Krishna presents Arjuna with His most supreme teaching: "Abandon all duties and take refuge in Me alone. I will liberate you from all sins; fear not." This is a powerful mantra which will help the devotee to effect total self-surrender if he constantly keeps before his mind the feeling: "I surrender myself to God." Those who repeat this with feeling will soon receive the grace of the Lord and be able to accomplish perfect self-surrender. The grace of the Lord cannot come to one who thinks and speaks of his own ability. God's grace descends on the very humble soul, who upholds that God does everything and knows that he is only an instrument in His hands.

The devotee who is ready to surrender everything to God realizes that He alone is acting through him, that He alone has given him all intelligence and opportunities. He does not take any credit for himself, but attributes everything to God's grace. One must surrender everything to Him and perform every action as an offering to Him to obtain His grace. Single-mindedness is an important factor in surrender. When the body, mind and ego are surrendered to the Lord, one realizes his oneness with Him. It is necessary to reduce oneself to zero before God. One should constantly take refuge in the Lord and in the names of the Lord. One should take refuge in His grace, in His lotus feet, and in the company of saints and mahatmas.

Maha kripa, the grace of the great ones, is necessary for spiritual progress. Kabir, Tulsidas, Sri Shankaracharya and

Guru Nanak have all written volumes on the glory of satsang with mahatmas. Faith in God slowly develops in those who are regular in satsang. In fact, it is said that bhakti cannot be cultivated without association with saints. Satsang destroys all worldly attachments, desires and cravings. Even a moment's contact with saints and sages is highly beneficial. There is no difference between God and a realized saint or *bhagavata*; both are identical. There is no hope of overhauling the old, vicious impressions of a worldly person without the satsang of mahatmas.

Prayer for grace

One should not pray for earthly goods or for heavenly pleasures, but for total surrender to His grace: "Thy will be done, My Lord! I surrender to you absolutely! I want nothing," should be one's prayer. One should kneel down and pray that His righteousness may descend upon the souls of everyone, that His light may illumine the hearts of all leaders and pave the way for the peace of all humanity. There are no problems that cannot be solved, no sufferings that cannot be allayed, no difficulties that cannot be surmounted and no evil that cannot be overcome by prayer.

Prayer is communion with God, the miracle by which God's power flows into human veins. The breath which has been given by the Lord should be spent in prayer. After kneeling down and praying, the prayer should not cease upon arising. Prayer should be life long and life should be one long prayer. One should pray, not only for relief from pain and suffering, but also for the liberation of others from ignorance of the law of God. This is the true form that prayer takes in a virtuous life. One should greet the dawn of day and bid adieu to the setting sun with a prayer of thankfulness for the new day granted and for His Grace received. Thus shall one's life be blessed and His blessings will radiate to all around him.

When the storms of war and unrest gather, one should kneel down and pray. Abraham Lincoln, the greatest architect of freedom, has said: "I have been driven many times to my knees by the overwhelming conviction that I had nowhere else to go. My own wisdom and that of all about me seemed insufficient for the day." When the storms of lust and anger, vanity and viciousness, rage within the bosom, one should kneel down and pray. The Lord alone has power over the elements. In prayer is one's strength. One will be filled with His blessings, protected by His grace, shielded by His mercy and spurred on the spiritual path by His divine will.

Mystery and glory of divine will

The entire creation is the play of God. We are all so many toys in His hands. After tossing us about here and there, goading us to run hither and thither, and making us do various actions, He stands aloof and watches our success and failure, joy and sorrow. Tired of these worldly ways, the devotee seeks His lotus feet for rest and peace. Then He sweetly whispers into his ears that it was all His doing! It was only a means to bring you to Him, in complete surrender. When a long cherished dream is realized, it is because He willed it so. When it is smashed, even then it is because He willed it so! What a joke! "O my Beloved Lord and Master, Thy will be done! I want nothing in this world."

Divine will is mysterious, ever elusive, ever receding, subtle, inexpressible, invisible and yet all-pervading, knowable through intuition, devotion and purity. Who can know the divine will? Only one who has surrendered unreservedly to God can know it as the source, the substratum and the ultimate goal of life. He bows his head in all humility and sincerity at the lotus feet of the Lord and receives His grace. The divine will is displayed in every inch of creation. Who provides food for the little frog living in-between the strata of rocks? Who clothed fruits with skin to prevent contamination from outside? The description of His glories is endless.

Divine will is an eternal, unalterable law. One who surrenders his individual will at the feet of the Lord will know the divine will. But self-surrender must be total, ungrudging and unreserved. Through total, unreserved self-

surrender to the Lord, every moment of life, every action and thought becomes consecrated to God. *Atma nivedana*, self-surrender, is the highest rung on the ladder of yoga. God is immanent in this world and also transcendent. God creates the world and remains as its inner ruler. The first sloka of the *Ishavasya Upanishad* begins with: "All movable and immovable objects in this universe are indwelt by the Lord." In the *Kathopanishad* it says: "This God is hidden in all things." Only one who is able to truly surrender to Him is able to appreciate and live according to His Will.

The upanishadic seers have spoken very highly of the *dhira* or brave aspirants who place their entire existence in the divine will. One who has attained that has nothing more to long for. Such a devotee lives for Him and Him alone. When surrender is complete, God takes complete charge of the devotee and looks after his welfare. He reveals to him His play and His will in the world. The aspirant should strictly adhere to the will of God. He should not turn aside on account of hardships or egoistic inclinations. By following the divine will of inner revelation, the light will shine more and more, and will grow into a blazing fire of wisdom and union with God.

8

Guru-Disciple Relationship

Surrender to God is man's yearning to reach the highest and to become perfect. Samarpan liberates one from individual existence and installs one in the Absolute, in God or in Brahman. Without treading the path of surrender, worldly bondage cannot be broken. Samsara cannot cease as long as objects are used as a means of satisfaction for the individual self. Only when the disciple has been able to identify the whole universe with the Absolute Self can knowledge become an end in itself. Only then will duality be abolished and absolute surrender realized. However, the path of samarpan is very difficult to tread, so devotees are obliged to receive shelter and guidance from those who are able to lift them up to these highest levels.

Throughout the ages, the institution of the guru *parampara* or tradition has closely safeguarded and handed down the living experiences of the seers from generation to generation. In India, this has been regarded a most sacred task and the role of the great gurus has always been considered a divine mission. The ancients have deified the guru to strengthen man's wavering faith and to ensure the right *bhava* or inner attitude that is necessary for the fruition of all worship. The guru is the human witness to the Supreme Self, the counterpart of the Lord on earth. The guru offers the key to samarpan. He knows how to mould the disciple so that he can commune with the immortal Lord, who is otherwise invisible to the physical eye. Through surrender to the guru, the disciple attains knowledge of God.

The guru is the guarantee that worldly bound individuals will one day transcend the bondage of sorrow and death, and experience the consciousness of God, the Absolute or the Supreme Self. The guru represents the sublime, transcendental state, which he has attained. Therefore, surrender to the visible guru is verily direct worship and surrender to the Supreme Reality. Develop the vision that your guru is divinity personified. Behold the entire universe as a living guru, ever teaching you lessons of life! Worship the guru in all his forms, as Ishwara, the universe, and as your personal guru in human form. Therefore, surrender to guru is seeking shelter in the origin of knowledge, the source of power, the Lord of creation itself.

Who qualifies for discipleship?
The desire for self-surrender is the precondition of becoming a disciple. The surrender of the disciple to the guru is really the attempt of the individual soul to gain access to the universal Self. One must be a sincere aspirant to approach a guru. Correct understanding, non-attachment to worldly objects, serenity of mind, restraint of the senses, absence of base passions, faith in the guru and devotion to God are the necessary qualities which the aspirant must have. The foundation of discipleship is total, unconditional and absolute self-surrender to guru. Absolute faith in the thoughts, words and actions of the guru is the first rung on the ladder, and unwavering devotion to guru is the greatest factor.

The guru will impart spiritual instructions only to that aspirant who thirsts for liberation, who duly obeys the injunctions of the shastras, who has subdued his passions and senses, who has a calm mind, and who possesses virtuous qualities like mercy, cosmic love, patience, humility, endurance and forbearance. A neophyte cannot have God as guru to begin with; he must have a personal guru first and practise surrender to him. In order to have God as guru, one must have a pure mind, ethical perfection, and be above body-consciousness. Communion with God will fructify only when the disciple's mind becomes purified. The secrets are explained to those high-souled aspirants whose devotion to the Lord is great and whose devotion to the guru is as great as to the Lord, and they become illumined. Guru guides and inspires such devoted disciples from the innermost core of their being.

Living with the guru
Samarpan is a spiritual sadhana, a revelation of divinity; it cannot be taught by lectures or correspondence courses. Though God is everywhere, His presence cannot be felt by one who has not been endowed with the required faith and devotion to have the divine experience. The surest way to attain these qualities is to live under a preceptor for many years and lead a rigorous life of austerity, discipline, celibacy and deep meditation. The devotee's big ego makes the path of surrender most difficult. The force of habit is very strong and inveterate. To manage the ego demands relentless dedication to the selfless service of a guru. The guru will manifest within in proportion to the effacement of the ego. Therefore, the disciple should empty himself so that the guru may fill him.

The guru-disciple relationship is certain to remove the disturbing elements from the mind: self-justification, vanity, procrastination, obstinacy, fault-finding, evil company, dishonesty, arrogance, lust, anger, greed and egoism. The guru will help the disciple to control his emotions and passions. He will enable him to eliminate fear, ignorance, pessimism, confusion of mind, disease, despair and worry, and will give him the power to resist temptations. These great stumbling blocks on the path of surrender will be removed under the guru's direct guidance, and then the disciple will be fit to receive the guru's grace.

The disciple who really desires samarpan must be frank with himself and straightforward with his guru. One who cannot open his heart to his guru cannot benefit from his help. He remains stuck in his own self-created mire and cannot move along the divine path. The aspirant often feels helpless against the force of old habits, but if he surrenders to his guru, he will be provided with suitable ways to eradicate them. While living with his guru, he will learn how to introspect and discover his own weaknesses and strengths. The disciple should always adapt, adjust and accommodate in regard to the guru under all circumstances.

It is easy to tame a wild tiger, lion or elephant, it is easy to walk over fire or water, but it is impossible to surrender to God unless one is able to surrender to the lotus feet of the guru. One may study endless books on philosophy, deliver lectures throughout a global tour, remain in a Himalayan cave for thousands of years, practise pranayama for years on end, or remain in sirshasana for one's whole life. However, if one cannot surrender to the guru, one will not be able to surrender to God. The length of time taken for the disciple's spiritual illumination is directly proportionate to his capacity to surrender to the guru.

The guru teaches samarpan through personal example. The life of the guru is a living sermon for the sincere disciple. The day-to-day conduct of the guru is a living ideal for the disciple who is observant. By constant contact the disciple imbibes the virtues of his guru and is gradually moulded. The *Chhandogya Upanishad* describes how Indra stayed with his guru, Prajapati, for a period of one hundred and one years, serving him wholeheartedly. Only the guru knows the spiritual needs of his disciples. The mind of the guru, being nearest to the absolute condition of changeless existence, possesses limitless powers beyond imagination.

The guru gives *upadesha*, spiritual instructions, according to the disciple's temperament and evolution. These instructions should be kept secret. Discussion amongst disciples will lead to criticism of the guru and slackness in sadhana; there will be no spiritual progress. The disciple should follow the guru's guidance to the very letter, remembering that it is meant only for him. Other disciples will receive their guru upadesha and should follow that. The disciple should not impose the upadesha he has received upon others.

The seeker of liberation and immortality should serve, honour and adore the guru wholeheartedly. The greatest way to honour the guru is by closely emulating the lofty example that he embodies in his own life and conduct, and by striving to live up to the ideals that the guru loves. The guru is not pleased by praise or adoration, but by ceaseless aspiration, endeavour and struggle to adhere to those principles to which he has dedicated his life.

Sincerity, faith and obedience

The guru is identical with the supreme existence itself, and hence his guidance cannot be estimated by thought or intellect. The initiation of the disciple by the guru is a process of infusion of a supernormal force of spiritual consciousness into the grosser state of the disciple's mind. The initiation results in the dispelling of darkness and enlightening of the disciple's mind. The qualification for taking this initiation is the simple trio of sincerity, faith and obedience. The disciple should be sincere in his aspiration for perfection, not vague or half-hearted. He should have perfect faith in the one he has accepted as guru, not allowing a shadow of doubt to approach him.

When the disciple has absolute faith in his guru, he knows that the instructions received from him are for his highest good. He should be earnest in following them and thereby he will attain perfection. The disciple should be sincere in his practice of japa, meditation and study. He should surrender to the guru and depend on the guru. He should be understanding and practical. He should permeate himself with love for the guru and guru seva, and strive ceaselessly to mould himself along the lines of his teachings. This is the precious secret of all attainment, the key to the kingdom of God, and the direct path to perfection.

Faith gives confidence and trust in the guru's teachings; it is the means to absolute surrender. Faith is firm conviction of the truth of what is declared by the preceptor by way of testimony or authority, without any evidence or proof. The disciple who has faith in the guru does not argue, think, reason or cogitate; he simple obeys. The disciple should be deserving of the guru's grace before he desires to receive it. Guru's grace descends only upon those who are utterly humble and faithful to him. For aspirants endowed with unflinching faith, the guru-disciple relationship becomes the means to attain the very purpose of human existence: realization of transcendental consciousness.

Faith enables the disciple to place himself totally in the guru's hands and to follow his instructions implicitly. Such a disciple alone can evolve. The guru can inspire him to remove all the obstacles along the path of surrender. The guru cannot do sadhana for the disciple. He has to take each step on the spiritual path himself, but the guru is there to guide him if he has faith in him and in himself. The guru alone breaks the binding cords of attachment and releases the aspirant from the trammels of earthly existence.

Obedience is the sacred essence of the guru-disciple relationship. Obedience is the law of life for a disciple. Obedience to guru is reverence itself. Only the disciple who obeys his guru can have command over his lower self. Obedience is a precious virtue because it slowly roots out the ego, the arch-enemy on the path of self-realization. Obedience should be practical, wholehearted and actively persevering. True obedience to the guru neither procrastinates nor questions. A hypocritical disciple obeys his guru from fear. The true disciple obeys his guru unquestionably, with pure love for love's sake, considering it his sacred duty to do so.

Obedience to guru is the highest worship, far greater than worship with garlands and other outward manifestations of adoration. In order to attain samarpan, the highest state in spiritual life, obedience to the guru is a necessity and a blessing. The disciple should give up the delusive notions that to submit to the preceptor, to obey him and to carry out his instructions is a slavish mentality. The ignorant person thinks it beneath his dignity and against his freedom to submit to another's command, but such thinking is a grave blunder.

By reflecting carefully, one will understand that individual freedom is really abject slavery to the ego and vanity. Only one who attains victory over the mind and ego is truly free. He is the spiritual hero who attains self-surrender! By this submission he vanquishes his lower ego and realizes the bliss of infinite consciousness. Therefore, the disciple should obey the guru's every instruction implicitly and follow his teachings to the letter. One who is earnest in this will attain perfection. The highest attainment of spiritual life is achieved through the guru-disciple relationship.

Transformation of consciousness

Some compare the path of surrender with the effort required to empty the ocean with a blade of grass! The *Kathopanishad* says: "He is difficult to obtain and even to hear of. Even when heard of, He is not known by many." "Unless taught by a teacher, there is no way of knowing that which is subtler than the subtle and not to be argued about." Although the guru does not actually teach anything that is not already known, he shows the way to dig out the spiritual wealth that is buried under the ignorant mind of the disciple.

The guru is the gateway to transcendental consciousness, but the disciple has to enter through it. The guru is a help, but the actual task of practical sadhana falls on the disciple. The guru draws out the knowledge of the disciple from within by suitable methods. Even the nature of this act of drawing out knowledge is dependent on the ripeness or maturity of the disciple's mind and the ability of the preceptor. The receptivity of the disciple and the knowledge and capacity of the guru with whom he has come in contact are both to the same degree.

The disciple does not surrender to the guru for material gain, but to commune with the substratum of life, the grand consciousness that soars above the paltry grandeur of the universe. In order to effect conscious change in the mind of the disciple, the guru must either come down to the level of the disciple's mind or raise the mind of the disciple to his own state. The guru-disciple relationship is the science and art of mastering the mind. It includes every discipline: physical, mental, moral and spiritual, which leads to self-mastery and self-realization.

Two things are necessary for a beautifully finished idol or image. One is a perfect, faultless piece of marble and the second is an expert sculptor. The piece of marble should remain in the hands of the sculptor unconditionally in order to be carved and chiselled into a fine image. So, too, the disciple only has to purify and make himself like a faultless piece of marble. Then he must place himself under the expert guidance of his master and allow himself to be carved and chiselled into the image of God.

In order to surrender to the divine will, the disciple must become a personification of receptivity. He must empty himself of the petty ego-sense, and then all the treasures locked up in the bosom of nature will be his! The disciple should become as pure and unattached as a mountain breeze. All his thoughts, words and actions should be directed only towards God by moving every moment of his life towards the supreme state, just as a river constantly flows towards the ocean.

The lower nature of the mind must be thoroughly regenerated if the disciple is to attain total self-surrender. The aspirant says to his guru: "I want to practise yoga and enter samadhi. I want to sit at your feet. I have surrendered myself to you." But he does not want to change his lower nature, character, behaviour and conduct. The obstinate disciple clings to his old habits, preconceived notions, pet ideas, prejudices and selfish interests. All of these need to be given up, as they stand in the way of carrying out the teachings and instructions of the guru.

The essence of surrender lies in being able to live according to his teachings. The disciple who practises yoga according to the instructions of the guru can annihilate the ego without any difficulty, and easily crosses over the quagmire of samsara. If the disciple will not surrender to his personal guru, how will he submit to the Lord? The transformation of personality is not easy. The hard rajasic ego is the enemy of the sadhaka.

Service to guru
Guru seva is the surest and best sadhana to destroy arrogance and to dissolve the vicious ego. Just as a particular deadly germ can be annihilated only by a specific chemical germicide, even so to destroy ignorance and the sense of I-ness, this unique sadhana is the peerless specific. Service to the guru is the gravest 'mayacide' and 'egocide'. The selfish ego becomes quite powerless and no longer afflicts the fortunate soul who saturates himself with the spirit of seva. In the beginning the disciple should direct his whole attention towards the removal of selfishness by protracted service of the guru.

Selfless service to the guru is the key to transformation of the ego-sense. Service to guru breaks all the barriers. It helps to develop divine virtues, such as mercy, humility, obedience, love, faith, devotion, patience and sacrifice. It destroys jealousy, hatred and pride, and helps to overcome 'I-ness' and 'mine-ness'. The disciple should scrutinize his inner motives and serve the guru without any selfish end. Service to guru must be done without expectation of name, fame, power or wealth. Only then can he lose his little ego and surrender to God. When the disciple serves his guru with divine bhava, the barrier of individuality is dissolved.

The disciple lives to serve his guru. He watches for opportunities to serve without waiting for invitations. He volunteers for the guru's service and serves him humbly, willingly, unquestioningly, unassumingly, ungrudgingly, untiringly and lovingly. The more energy he spends in serving the guru, the more divine grace flows into him. One should not miss any opportunities to serve the divine teacher. One who serves the guru, serves the whole world. Service of guru is service to humanity, the self and the Divine!

Guru tests

The satguru communicates the secret essence of the Upanishads to his trusted disciples only after repeated entreaty and severe testing. He tests his disciples in various ways. The guru tests the disciple's faith to see if it is strong. He tests the heart and mind of the disciple to see if they have become pure. The disciple can strengthen his faith, cleanse his mind and purify his heart only through tests and tribulations. The heart must become pure and the faith unflinching by passing through trials again and again, just as gold is purified by passing it through the fire.

Sometimes the students who are being tested misunderstand the guru's intention and lose their faith in him. In days of yore, the tests set by the guru were very severe. Once Gorakhnath asked some of his students to climb up a tall tree and throw themselves down head first onto a sharp trident. The faithless students remained at the base of the tree, but one faithful student climbed up the tree at once with lightning speed and hurled himself downwards. He was protected by the invisible hand of Gorakhnath, and had immediate self-realization.

Once Guru Govind Singh decided to test his students and said: "My dear disciples! If you have real devotion towards me, let six of you come forward and give me your heads. Then you can have success in your spiritual attempt." Two faithful disciples came forward and offered their heads to the guru, while the rest stood back. Guru Govind Singh took these two inside the camp and cut off the heads of two goats instead.

True discipleship

The spiritual path is not like writing a thesis for a Master of Arts degree; it follows a different line altogether. The help of a teacher is necessary at every moment. Discipleship awakens the dormant facilities necessary for accessing universal consciousness. It is most necessary in one's journey along the spiritual path. The guru guides, inspires and blesses the disciple. He transmits, transforms and spiritualizes him. The guru and disciple become one, and divine communion follows. Every disciple worships the guru in his own way. There are disciples who worship the guru by identifying him with God. Through their act of total resignation, the guru becomes the channel through which the grace of God flows. God becomes visible for them in the form of guru and works tangibly in the form of a human being.

Young disciples often become self-sufficient, arrogant and self-assertive. They may not wish to carry out the orders of the guru or to have a guru at all. They want independence from the very beginning. They think they are in the *turiya avastha* or superconscious state when they do not even know the ABC of spirituality or truth. They mistake licentiousness and having their own way for freedom. They lose faith in the efficacy of sadhana and the existence of God. They wander about in a happy-go-lucky manner, without any aim, from Kashmir to Gangotri and from Gangotri to Rameshwaram, talking some nonsense from the scriptures on the way and posing as *jivanmuktas*, liberated beings. This is a serious and lamentable mistake, and for this reason they do not grow.

One must bend down in order to drink water from the tap. Even so, the disciple must be an embodiment of humility and meekness to drink the spiritual nectar of immortality that flows from the holy lips of the guru. One needs an empty heart, clear of all cravings, to fully benefit from the grace of the guru. Unless a person is blessed with exceptionally good understanding, discrimination and spiritual samskaras, he cannot grasp the meaning and significance of meditation on God and true spiritual life. When the guru imparts spiritual instructions, the disciple is not benefited if he does not pay attention and bolts the door of his heart.

The grace and blessings of the guru are very necessary, but the work must be done by the disciple. The guru will only tell his disciple the method of knowing the truth, the path that leads to the unfolding of intuition. If the disciple carries out his spiritual instructions implicitly, he will gain the knowledge of truth. Therefore, he should carefully follow the instructions of the guru. *Anubhava* or *aparoksha*, direct intuitive knowledge, can only be realized by one's own experience, just as a hungry person must eat for himself in order to satisfy his hunger.

There are disciples who want to lead a life of ease and expect to receive the grace of mahatmas. There are disciples who do not do any kind of tapasya or sadhana, and want a magic pill to instantly put them into samadhi. There are disciples who want worldly comforts and realization in one and the same cup, but this is not possible! The disciple cannot enter the spiritual path that leads to communion with God unless he is able to surrender to the divinity of the guru. The best disciple is like petrol or spirit. Even from a great distance he will instantly react to the spark of the guru's *upadesha*, or guidance. The second class disciple is like camphor. A torch awakens his inner spirit and kindles the fire of spirituality in him. The third class of disciple is like coal. The guru has to take great pains in order to awaken the spirit in him. The fourth class of disciple is like a plantain stem. No efforts will have any effect on him, whatever the guru may do; he remains cold and inert.

In order to become a better disciple, the eightfold limbs of the guru-disciple relationship should be observed and practised.

1. A sincere aspiration to know God
2. Prostrating with humility to the guru
3. Perfect obedience in carrying out the guru's commands
4. Performing selfless service to the guru as a *nishkama* yogi, without expectation of fruits
5. Identifying the guru with the Absolute; seeing God and guru as one
6. Worshipping the lotus feet of the guru with bhava and devotion
7. Surrender or dedication of one's life to the divine mission of the guru
8. Meditation on the holy feet of the guru to obtain his benign grace.

Guru is a form of divine grace

The *Shvetashvatara Upanishad* says: "In that great one, who has supreme devotion to God and as much devotion to guru as God, does the Truth become illumined." Teachers of real spiritual enlightenment, who can lead the disciple to realization of the truth, are very rare. To be a saint or a guru who dispels the inner darkness, one must have the command from God. Thus, the effect of such saintly company is unerring and infallible. These great souls generally hide their greatness, and their guidance is difficult to obtain. But the Lord brings the guru and the disciple together in a mysterious way. Through His grace only, the company of guru and saints is obtained.

The guru acts under the guidance of the Lord. The guru is God's instrument and appears only through the grace of the Lord. He transmits spiritual power to the disciple through instruction, look, touch or thought. The guru's grace descends only upon those disciples who are earnestly struggling on the path and thirsting for realization. A disciple who has earned great merits by strenuous endeavours in the present life or previous ones will be able to recognize the divine greatness of a guru and obtain his grace. The ignorant person impedes the path of grace by his conceit, arrogance and egoism. The lazy and indolent have no chance of obtaining the grace of a great soul.

The disciple should always act upon the guru's instructions. Only then will he deserve his blessings and will his blessings do everything. The disciple's surrender to the guru and the guru's grace are interrelated. Surrender draws down the guru's grace and the grace of guru makes the surrender complete. The guru's grace works in the form of sadhana in the aspirant. If a disciple sticks to the path tenaciously, this is the grace of guru. If he resists when temptation assails him, this is the grace of guru. If people receive him with love and reverence, this is the grace of the guru. If he obtains all bodily wants, this is the grace of the guru. If he gets encouragement and strength when he is in despair and despondency, this is the grace of the guru. If he overcomes body consciousness and rests in his own *ananda swaroopa*, blissful essence, this is the grace of the guru.

The disciple should feel his guru's grace at every step and be sincere and truthful to him. At the same time, he must remember that realization cannot come to him as a miracle performed by the guru. All great ones have had their teachers and done their sadhana. Lord Krishna asks Arjuna to develop *vairagya*, dispassion, and *abhyasa*, uninterrupted, constant spiritual practice. He does not say to him, "I will give you *mukti*, liberation, now." Therefore, the disciple should abandon the wrong notion that the guru will give him samadhi and mukti. He will have to strive, purify, meditate and realize it for himself.

All seekers of truth should recognize the deep implications of a life dedicated to the cause of Truth and God-realization, and seek the protection of a guru if they are to have real success in spiritual sadhana. All sophistry, ostentation, learning and conceit have to be cast off before the disciple approaches the great sage. The disciple should not feel that he has an independent personality or mission different from his guru. In fact, the personality of the disciple should be effaced if the wisdom of the teacher is to illumine him.

Samarpan

From the teachings of Swami Satyananda Saraswati

In the life of any individual, especially devoted and dedicated sannyasins, it is the moment of dedication, the moment of surrender, which is the inspiration to guide them through their lives. During the 1993 Tyag Golden Jubilee World Yoga Convention in Munger, Swami Satyananda sent the following message:

> *I send my good wishes for the convention. You call it Tyag Jayanti. I call it Samarpan Muhurat, the moment of dedication. It was that time, an auspicious moment in my life, which I experienced fifty years ago in the presence of my guru, Swami Sivanandaji Maharaj. To this day, I have always remembered it as a great moment of dedication.*

9

Origin of Samarpan

In the beginning, there was nothing, not even creation. There was only an all-pervasive, unmanifest consciousness, known in the scriptures as *Para Brahman*, the transcendental nature. In this calm state of consciousness, the first thought arose: "Let me become many." From this thought emerged another identity, known as Shiva. This first movement in consciousness, Shiva, was an inherently good, just and auspicious force. Shiva, however, was not alone; it was a combination of all the forces, including Shakti. Just as strength is contained in the body, oil in a sesame seed and fire in a piece of wood, Shakti is contained in Shiva in the original state. In order to multiply or 'become many', the first thought had to divide again, and thus manifested a separate identity of Shakti. Therefore, the first form to emerge was the half-male, half-female avatar of *Ardhanarishwara*, in which the principles of Shiva and Shakti were both identifiable.

Five attributes of Shiva

In tantra, creation begins with the emergence of Shiva from the unmanifest consciousness. The transcendental Shiva consciousness has five major attributes or powers: sarva kartritwa roopa, sarva tattwa roopa, nityatwa roopa, poornatwa roopa and vyapatattwa roopa.

1. The first attribute, *sarva kartritwa roopa*, refers to the creative force, the power possessing the capacity to create

an entire universe from nothing. *Sarva* means total; *kartritwa* means doership, the capacity to perform.
2. The second attribute, *sarva tattwa roopa*, refers to the fact that all the *tattwas* or elements necessary for the emergence of new identity are inherent in that invisible form, just as a tree is contained in a seed. The tree cannot be seen in the seed, but one is aware of the seed's potency to create a tree.
3. The third attribute is *nityatwa roopa*, Shiva as the energy which is *nitya*, eternal, continuous and unbroken.
4. The fourth attribute is *poornatwa roopa*, the attribute of wholeness, completeness. This concept is referred to in the Shanti mantra of the *Ishavasya Upanishad*: "*Om poornamadah poornamidam poornaat poornamudachyate, poornasya poornamaadaaya poornamevaavashishyate.*" Everything has emerged from *poornata*, completeness.
5. The fifth attribute is *vyapatattwa roopa*, the quality of being all-pervasive.

Tantra believes that humankind has its origin in the all-pervasive Shiva consciousness. In the journey of evolution, however, the individual has forgotten his origin and true identity. There is identification with the name and form given in a particular lifetime, but that is not the true identity. The true identity has been forgotten and cannot be regained until the individual fully surrenders to that pure state of consciousness.

Five components of the individual self
The created identity of an individual is composed of different states of consciousness, which are like invisible coverings on the individual self, the *jiva*, embodied in the physical, gross body. These five coverings are known as *kanchukas*, aspects of energy which restrict consciousness and create the notion of duality.
1. The first covering on the individual self is *kala*, manifestation, which limits the creative power of individual consciousness. Everything that is generated through the senses, the mind, thoughts or ideas, whatever manifests from or within an individual, whether a building or an idea, is kala.

2. The second covering is *vidya*, knowledge which is a product of the senses and mind. One is able to perform actions and duties with the aid of vidya. Without vidya, kala or manifestation has no meaning. Creation is guided by knowledge.
3. The third covering is *raga*, attachment, association and identification, which creates like and dislike. Every human being exists in the state of raga, whether external or internal. Raga could manifest as an association with one's parents or with a belief. All the attachments, associations and identifications which form a part of one's individual identity come in the category of raga.
4. The fourth component of individual identity is *niyati*, destiny. Everything in the universe has its own destiny, which is fulfilled in due course. A seed cannot convert itself into an animal and an egg will not become a rose bush. Water is destined to flow and quench thirst, and fire is destined to give out heat and burn. The *swabhava*, natural character, represents the destined effect of any object or being. An individual can observe his destiny only at the final moment of life, when he may obtain a perspective on the direction his life took, and realize whether there was evolution or regression, whether he was happy and content or struggled and suffered. That last moment discloses one's destiny in a given life, but while going through it, the individual does not know what lies in store.
5. The fifth covering on the individual self is *kaalatwa*, containment, which limits perpetual existence by creating the notion of time. A human being is contained, life is contained and experiences are contained. One only lives from this point to that point, from birth to death. This limit is defined as kaala.

The concept of samarpan

If the purpose of existence is reunification of the individual self with the higher Self, then what is the simplest way to achieve it? How can the limitations of individual identity, the five kanchukas, be managed so that the purpose of human incarnation is attained? It is said in the scriptures that samarpan is the best possible method to achieve this purpose. The process of surrender, or the sadhana of samarpan as visualized by the rishis, the ancient seers, covers the entire aspect of creation.

Samarpan means 'total offering'. *Sam* means 'total' and *arpan* means to 'offer', 'submit', 'relinquish' or 'surrender'. Samarpan is a notion that denotes duality. One offers something to something else. What does one offer, and to whom is it offered? What does one surrender, and to whom is it surrendered? One's individual identity is offered, the particular composition of the five kanchukas, to the five powers of Shiva.

To the sarva kartritwa roopa of Shiva, the creative force, one relinquishes the kala element, the individual identity, mind, thoughts, all that manifests through one. To the sarva tattwa roopa, the potency required for creation, one submits the vidya element, reasoning and knowledge. To the nityatwa roopa, the eternal attribute of creation, one relinquishes raga, attachments and individual identifications. To the poornatwa roopa, the wholeness and completeness of creation, one offers the niyati element, everything that is destined. To the vyapatattwa roopa, the all-pervading, omnipresent attribute of consciousness, one surrenders the kaalatwa element, the limited, restricted nature.

By following the process of samarpan, the continual struggle one undergoes with a limited identity can be managed, whether the it is for happiness and satisfaction, or for social, financial and emotional gain. Through samarpan, the devotee flows with the guiding force behind creation, becoming one with the cosmic and universal flow. Whether God is perceived as being separate or experienced within, one has to surrender to that pure consciousness to be able to commune with it. Whether divinity is perceived as external or internal, both require surrender. This is how the idea emerged of offering back the five kanchukas to the five attributes of Shiva. This is the origin of the concept of samarpan.

10
Culmination of all Sadhana

In every form of spiritual practice, the last stage is where the practitioner has offered his individual identity to a higher force, so that he can merge with it. In every sadhana, samarpan is the final experience of the *jiva*, the individual self, before becoming one with the *Paramatma*, the Supreme Self.

In bhakti yoga, for example, nine stages have been defined: *shravana*, hearing God's stories and satsang; *kirtan*, singing His glories; *smarana*, constant remembrance of His name and presence; *padaseva*, service of His feet; *archana*, ritual worship of God with or without form; *vandana*, prostration and prayer to the Lord; *dasya*, cultivating the attitude of a servant to God; *sakhya*, cultivating the attitude of a friend to God; and *Atma nivedana*, complete surrender of the self. The final stage, Atma nivedan, is samarpan, yielding completely to God. In the *Ramacharitamanas*, it has been said: "By systematic practice of *navadha bhakti*, the nine stages of bhakti, a point of total self-surrender can be attained." In the final stage of bhakti there is fusion, total identification and oneness with the object of contemplation, along with dissolution of the external nature. This is samarpan.

In raja yoga there are eight stages to achieve union: yama, niyama, asana, pranayama, pratyahara, dharana, dhyana and samadhi. The last stage of samadhi is *asmita*, where the ego and the sense of individuality are completely dissolved; the lower consciousness is transformed and merged with the higher consciousness. This, too, is samarpan. Jnana yoga reaches its culmination when there is full experiential knowledge of the merger with higher consciousness. Similarly, when karma yoga is perfected, the ego is eliminated; then the feeling is: *Na ham karta, Hari karta, Hari karta hi kevalam* – "I am not the doer, the supreme consciousness is the performer." When this total surrender of the karmas happens, without any ego-identification or sense of gain, then purity of mind, action, speech and thought is experienced. Such a state of purity ultimately takes one to unknown dimensions.

Ultimate point of evolution
Samarpan is the experience of union and also of dissolution of the outer nature, which is the aim of all spiritual sadhana. As the devotee passes through different stages of sadhana, he experiences altered states of consciousness, behaviour and human interaction. Ultimately, one is led to the state where individuality dissolves into the cosmic energy. Samarpan, therefore, is the highest state of mind that can be developed and experienced. Consciously surrendering one's entire existence into the hands of God is the highest state a spiritual aspirant can aspire for. It is the culmination of *jnana*, knowledge, the culmination of *bhakti*, devotion, and the culmination of *karma*, performance. It happens when jnana, bhakti and karma fuse into one stream and are directed to the fulfilment of the divine will. Samarpan is the ultimate point of evolution. It is the point where one consecrates oneself, where one dedicates oneself to the fulfilment of a greater purpose, which is in the bosom of the higher will.

Lord Krishna states in the *Bhagavad Gita* that the karma yogi sees inaction in action and action in inaction (4:18); the jnana yogi sees one soul abiding in all living beings (6:29); and the bhakti yogi see one God in everything and experiences Him everywhere (6:30). Having realized non-action, a karma yogi has nothing to do, so nothing remains to be known and there is nothing to be attained. Having realized the Self, the *Atma*, nothing remains to be known for a jnana yogi, so nothing remains to be done or attained. Similarly, having attained God, nothing remains to be done or known for a bhakti yogi. On achieving the goal through these three yogas, the aspirant's self-conscious ego is completely dissolved, and the essential element remains, which is realized. Then there remains no difference in the practices of these aspirants. Having become the spiritual sadhana, an aspirant is transformed into the spiritual goal. The last stage of all the different yogas aims to bring the aspirant towards the experience of merging with the cosmic or universal consciousness.

As long as one does not completely surrender to God with head, heart and hands, one cannot commune with Him fully. Samarpan means offering, dedicating and surrendering all practices and acts to the Supreme Guru, as well as renouncing the results and fruits thereof. It is the state when one thinks, "My Lord, before You I do not exist. I cannot think; You think through me. I leave the choices of my life in Your hands." Then He lives in one's heart like a constant light. This is also called *Atma samarpan*, self-surrender.

When the devotee submits entirely all that belongs to him, all will be given by Him. The secret of this gain is hidden in giving totally the things of fleeting value against the thing of absolute value. When one gives everything of oneself, one not only gains Him, but also regains oneself. The sea tells the river, "If you want to become one with me, you will have to merge yourself in me and lose your individuality." In the same way, if the aspirant wants to attain Him, he will have to offer everything to Him. As soon as one offers oneself to Him, the yoga of meditation manifests in full.

Eternal connection

To surrender oneself, one's personality, future, wealth, name and everything else is not a small matter. This surrender is our connection with eternity. It should never be questioned, and never brought down to a gross level. In every science there are dedicated souls who surrender their lives to the perfection of their field. Yogis retire into seclusion for a period of time, not only to perfect themselves, but to experience their souls. These divine souls work with a higher purpose, just like the scientists who work in their laboratories with such total dedication to their research that they are unmindful of the rest of the world.

Samarpan is attaching the mind to God completely and leaving everything else out. When the mind is attached to a man or woman, it is passion; when it is attached to money, it is greed; but when the mind is attached to God alone, it is samarpan. If this is what one wants, then all the feelings and attachments that are now flowing in different directions should be directed towards one focus, the Divine Presence. Anyone who wants to surrender to divinity should do everything that purifies the mind and aims at self-purification. He should gather together his emotions from all other relationships and direct them towards God.

Samarpan is a state of consciousness in which not even a speck of the mind functions, and this state is experienced only by one's Self. Summing up the teachings of the *Bhagavad Gita*, the Lord says (18:66): "Abandon all duties and surrender to Me alone. Fear not, for I shall liberate you from all sins." The Lord finally asks the devotee to lay down all burdens at His feet. Total surrender is when one yields to Him, not due to pressure of circumstances, but voluntarily with hands folded, head bowed, ego surrendered and heart divinized.

11

An Evolutionary Process

Applying samarpan in one's life is not easy. It is easy to say, "I surrender to God, I leave everything in the hands of God," but living samarpan is a totally different matter. In the normal course of events, an individual is not in control of his life. Society and worldly relationships decide how he must live, function, think and behave. One lives in society and is therefore forced to live according to the dictates of society. Similarly, the dictates of relationships must also be adhered to. Decisions are not made independently even if the individual thinks they are. He is not master of his own will.

When one is not master of his own will, why is it difficult to let go of it? Due to ignorance and arrogance, due to the ego and negativity. When these factors arise, it means that the individual is not tackling his personality appropriately. If one dealt with the *kanchukas*, the five limitations of individual identity, with the conviction, "I have to let go of all I am holding on to," the personality would follow suit.

A sadhana to perfect

Ultimately, the aspirant has to arrive at the unadulterated state of samarpan. It is, however, a process, a sadhana to perfect. Just as it takes time for water placed in a refrigerator to freeze and become ice, in the same way, transformation of this mind into a peaceful mind has to happen in stages.

Everyone reacts to life differently. Some people submit and surrender to circumstances, others fight with circumstances. Those who possess higher knowledge and know that existence itself is the will of God do not worry. One's attitude to life depends on the kind of person one is. When there are desires and passions, we fight with life. When there are no desires and no passions, nothing to gain and nothing to lose, when one does not depend on worldly things, only then one can surrender to God. That is the best way. When the devotee is exhausted, he may offer everything to Him. This state comes as the very last point in spiritual life, for it is the most difficult part of surrender. This level of surrender should happen automatically, naturally, without any force or strain; it cannot be an intellectual decision.

It is not easy to restructure our whole way of thinking, the total philosophy of one's life. The aspirant is trying to achieve this in samarpan, but he is not always successful. He will often stumble and fall, but this does not matter as long as he is able to pick himself up and continue walking. Eventually, the light will come. In the eleventh chapter of the *Bhagavad Gita*, Arjuna asks Lord Krishna: "Lord, please show me your cosmic form, so that I may see and know you as God." Lord Krishna replies: "It is not easy to see the divine form with these limited eyes, with this limited mind and awareness." Arjuna persists and finally Krishna relents and shows Arjuna His cosmic form. But as soon as it appears, Arjuna has a mind-exploding experience and he cries out in terror: "Lord, remove this experience, it is too frightening. I want to see you in the human form which I can understand."

Preparation is necessary in spiritual life. There is no point awakening the cosmic experience until one is ready to handle it. If one prepares the ground, receives initiation from a guru, attempts to practise surrender even a little bit, and takes vows for sadhana, then one has already become a medium, a good conductor of His thoughts. Gradually one's sense consciousness and body consciousness will be suspended; gradually one's mental consciousness will also be suspended. Slowly one's ego consciousness will be suspended, and then one's experiences of samskaras will be suspended. Finally, when the gross, the subtle and the causal bodies are withdrawn, He will either descend or enter into one. His original essence will remain unchanged while being expressed through the devotee and will be seen by others also. Water appears red in a red vessel, yellow in a yellow vessel and green in a green one. The real colour is seen only when the colour of the vessel and the water are identical. When the dew drop slips into the sea, a great miracle takes place: the miracle of the sea entering the dew drop.

Preparing the ground

The aspirant can prepare for the experience of samarpan by living a spiritual life. The first requirement is an environment where the influence of the five kanchukas, the invisible limitations on consciousness, is minimized. One must seek such an environment to refresh oneself, rephrase one's thoughts and ideas, revitalize and relive one's aspirations. It must be a place where one can reconnect with one's individual soul in order to connect with the transcendental consciousness.

An ashram is such a place. It offers an environment away from the seat of attachments, represented by *kala, raga, vidya, niyati* and *kaala*, manifestation, wisdom, attachment, destiny and time. Continuous association with an ashram, where spiritual life is practised and spiritual teachings are given and lived, will release one from the hooks of the kanchukas and lead to increased self-awareness.

The second requirement of samarpan is a guide or guru. Under the guru's guidance the whole structure of consciousness is transformed. The disciple then arrives at the stage where he begins to realize the great cosmic nature, the law of the Divine. After this, life becomes smooth-sailing. There is no more pain or pleasure. Inner life is totally changed, but outer life remains the same.

The concept of having faith and placing trust in a guru to guide one through life's experiences has existed in India from time immemorial. No other religion or philosophy in the world has spoken about this concept. The spiritual tradition in India is such that people have respect for and faith in their elders and look up to them to provide the right samskaras and inspiration. Therefore, placing one's trust in a guru is not a problem, it is not difficult to bow one's head with respect in front of an elder who can inspire and lead one to improve. The guru plays an important role in teaching the process of samarpan. By practising surrender to the guru and observing the reality of one's quest, the aspirant reaches the point of surrender to the divine will. While the ashram fine-tunes the kala and raga aspects, the guru fine-tunes the vidya, niyati and kaala aspects. Therefore, both the ashram and the guru play an important role in learning how to let go.

One has to let go. Apart from living in an ashram or associating with a guru, the process of letting go also happens with the practices of yoga and meditation, as they allow the aspirant to observe his associations and attachments. *Japa*, repeating one's mantra or the name of God, is an invaluable aid. The mantra should be repeated first thing every morning and before retiring at night, or whenever possible. While repeating the mantra, one must feel: "Although I do not see God, I know He is here." When the intellect begins to interrupt the flow of this feeling, one must contradict its every suggestion.

On completing the japa, one should make the resolve, "Let my devotion increase just as the moon expands to become full." This should be one's only sankalpa. The only prayer, repeated day after day, every morning and every night, should be, "Let my love and faith for You be greater than it was yesterday. Let me feel Your presence in the conscious, subconscious and unconscious realms. Wherever I am, let me feel Your Divine Being."

The difficulty in meditation is that the inner mind cannot grasp an object that it does not love. If one sticks to the guru mantra, it will give everything one prays for. Japa is meant to awaken the spiritual power, while prayer is to direct that power to a particular and desired end. Hence, one can pray at the end of japa, concentration or meditation practice. The aspirant's effort is aimed at rendering the mind waveless, calm, serene and infinite by one-pointed perception of the form. This becomes possible when love for God is coupled with yoga.

Role of bhakti

When we let go of something, we have to then move on to something else. This is where bhakti comes in. In the Indian tradition, bhakti marga is considered the easiest path to samarpan. Swami Sivananda used to say, "Bhakti marga is the easiest, safest, cheapest, quickest and best path." As the *vasanas*, desires, of the world are dropped, the vasanas of the Divine have to be awakened. Worldly vasanas have to be replaced with divine ones. One cannot be free from desire until the very end of existence as an individual soul.

However, a destructive desire can be replaced with a creative one, a restrictive desire transformed into an expansive one. By repeating the mantra and the sankalpa every day, the feeling of bhakti will arise from deep within and grow day by day. Bhakti can become a major support in the perfection of surrender. Like the saints and sages who sang and wrote about the glory of the Supreme in their devotional songs and poetry, the devotee will experience bhakti in every sphere of existence and know the exquisite feeling of unity.

Tulsidas says at the end of the *Ramacharitamanas*:

Forswearing the perversity of my soul,
I have chanted the glorious, holy and purifying exploits of Sri Rama.
This worship alone has secured my redemption;
My delusion, infatuation and impurity is now
Brimful with the water of love.
O Jewel of Raghu's race,
Men who devoutly take a plunge into your Manasa lake
Are never scorched by the burning rays of the sun of worldly illusion.

Another important factor is trust. Without trust, one will remain afraid. If there is trust, there is the knowledge that we will be taken care of. The devotee knows he is loved, he can feel it, and that is very important. It is not just a technique. Everyone is loved because they are part of the whole. To be able to deal with trying situations requires absolute trust and devotion. Devotion is the nature of the strength within. Devotion and trust fuel one's strength and allow one to cope. Devotion to God, love for God, is the ultimate sadhana on the road to samarpan.

God's grace
Ultimately, it is the *bhavana*, the inner feeling, that counts. All the methods written about samarpan, whether in the *Bible*, the *Bhagavad Gita* or the Upanishads are elucidated because man cannot remain inactive. The basic framework of how to develop spiritual life within has been given in the yogic, tantric and vedic traditions, but ultimately nothing except supreme love will immerse one in the Divine. The final union between the individual and the Divine rests in the mercy of God's grace. There is no known method to obtain God's grace. He will meet the devotee only if He wishes to, not because the devotee wishes to meet Him. God's grace is the link between man and Divinity. This must be remembered. He will reveal Himself only if He wants to, not because the aspirant has tried all the methods. To know how to commune with Him, one has to ask Him and pray to Him, "Show me the path, lead me on to it. I have no mental, physical or moral strength unless you bless me." Even the form in which God's grace appears, the form in which He reveals Himself or inspires one should be left to Him.

God is not a matter for the intellect. On that basis, one will fail for centuries, for thousands of lives. God is captivated by bhavana, feelings. It is not the bhavana of an academic or intellectual. It is the feeling that comes when one throws away all sense of superiority and ego, and says, "I am not an academic, scientist, author, teacher to so many disciples, or a pontiff. I am nothing. I abandon all supports and take refuge in You alone."

All that can be done to attain the state of samarpan is prepare oneself through whatever means to receive God's grace. One should awaken *bhakti*, devotion, develop *vairagya*, detachment, renounce worldly existence and perfect the yamas and niyamas. One should practise sadhana to purify the mind, empty oneself and develop a sattwic nature. One should practise *swadhyaya*, self-study, enquire into the nature of God and the purpose of existence, do japa of God's name, practise ascetic observances, be cordial to people and do all one can to become capable of participating in all the events of nature. One should find a genuine guru who knows the path to surrender. Little by little one should try to transform the values of life. Make resolves to surrender one aspect of the ego and then another, and keep revising them. Finally, remind yourself every day that the ultimate purpose of life is to abandon everything and surrender to the Divine. However, to be able to attain this highest resolve, the initial purpose must be to clean the road, to light the path and make the journey itself.

How samarpan is expressed eventually depends on the individual. There is no set path because each individual is different. If an intellectual and a bhakta are given the same instruction, the intellectual will think twice about it, while the bhakta will simply listen and act on it. The application of samarpan depends on how one uses one's convictions. Ultimately, samarpan means removal of the five coverings or kanchukas and offering them to, or merging oneself with, the transcendental, transformative consciousness.

Surrender to the divine will is inevitable

The individual soul, the *jivatma*, is always trying to attain and merge with *Paramatma*, the Supreme Being. There are two paths of evolution. One is *pravritti*, where involvement is in the world, in normal social. In this path, evolution follows its natural course. The other path is *nivritti*, pursuing a desire to obtain freedom and liberation. It is the path of self-observation, harmonization and samarpan; it is the path of experiencing spirituality in life.

There comes a point in human evolution when the urge to surrender to the divine will comes naturally. This is the point when the aspirant begins to realize that his individual soul is different from his gross and subtle body, and it is when he reaches a turning point in spiritual life. Now he begins to identify with his pure inner nature, the all-pervading, universal consciousness. Until then everything is guided by the ego: thoughts are guided by the ego, expectations are motivated by the ego, efforts are energized by the ego, reactions and identifications are associated with the ego. This is the point when, completely exhausted, the aspirant lets go of everything and places his life, with all humility, in the hands of the divine will. After trying to control the mind and passions for years without success, when all personal efforts have failed, when one realizes the foolishness of thinking things happened due to one's own efforts – at that time one may completely surrender, and say, "Do what You like. I have tried my best and lost. I realize that I can do nothing without You." Then there is an awakening, which only comes when one has totally surrendered.

Now the aspirant begins to be emptied of the individual ego, and is able to become an instrument of the Divine and live according to the divine will. Until then, surrender is not possible because the ego is a barrier between the individual and the Divine. Now the devotee seeks a means to consciously allow surrender to happen, for when one is thirsty for God, one cannot sit idle. Now God also appears to assist the devotee, but in which form it is not known.

It is inevitable that every individual soul will reach this state of evolution. Even if one does nothing, ultimately one will surrender to God, because that is the purpose of human existence. The individual is not really responsible for any awakening; it is Nature or God who is accomplishing everything. In tantra there is a collection of prayers called

Devi Aparadha Kshamapana Stotram. The opening verse says: "Mother, I do not know mantra, I do not practise yantra, I do not know how to pray, I do not know how to invoke you, I do not know how to meditate on you, and I do not know what your glories are. But I know that if I follow you, all my agonies will be redeemed." Similar verses follow, and the prayer concludes with, "No, I do not have to do anything." This is the tantric view: "I do not have to do anything. I have come and I am able to touch your feet. I am pure." The philosophy of the *Bhagavad Gita* is identical to tantric philosophy. Lord Krishna's final advice to Arjuna (18:66) is: "Leave everything and take shelter in Me." This means abandoning the dharma of prakriti, of the senses, mind, heart, intellect and emotions, leaving them all and fixing the mind on the Lord within. This is the evolutionary process of samarpan.

If samarpan is not the ultimate purpose of life, then life has no meaning. Human life has no other purpose. One may engage in any type of work and live however one likes. However, if one knows the goal of life, the purpose of human existence, then one's arrival in this world will have been successful and one may not need to come again.

12

Awakening Positive Forces

Surrender is difficult to practise, whether to God or anyone else. Even if one sincerely applies oneself, certain thoughts arise, certain influences affect the belief, doubt creeps in, questioning begins, and one falls prey to the influences of the mind. Two thousand years ago Christ's disciples had to face doubt, and today's spiritual aspirants will also have to face confusion and doubt. People say one should love, but loving is not easy. People say one should obey, but obedience is not easy. People say one should have pure intentions, but pure intentions are not easy. People say one should surrender, but surrender is not easy.

It has been said in the *Srimad Bhagavatam*: "The secret of your success is that you have dedicated yourself, you have surrendered yourself, but the moment you lose faith and forget your aim, you will succumb to doubts, anger, jealousy, passion, greed, delusion, fear, etc. Do not invite these dark forces of ego, because with them in your mind you will not be able to exercise His divine will. All mental arguments are invalid and useless. Remember, the secret of your success is that you have surrendered your ego. Worldly love and divine love cannot co-exist."

The path of samarpan is the path of the brave, of those who have realized that God is all and that by surrendering to Him, they will lose their limited self and gain the Supreme Self. Surrender is not an act of escapism, not a negation or rejection of life. It is rectifying the negative notions and impressions that have formed over lifetimes due to worldly attachments. It is the path for those who wish to become free from passion, desire and illusion. Samarpan is the path for those who want divinity alone.

Make the choice

There are aspirants who are free and independent, and deeply interested in spiritual life. They know the glory of *tyaga*, renunciation, and do not crave money, passion, name, fame and power. Yet something prevents them from renouncing what they know to be temporary and embracing what they believe to be permanent. They know that the ambitions they failed to fulfil in worldly life will be realized by taking to the path of renunciation. Yet they do not surrender.

There are two reasons for this state. Such aspirants are not certain whether samarpan will bless them with all they have been aspiring for. Some unseen fear lurks within, and this fear comes only after they start to think twice about their notion of surrender. Many such aspirants eventually lose their inspiration due to the unconscious forces of jealousy and other complicated ego factors. Those who remain on the path continue to imagine the glory of renunciation while living in the abyss of fear and uncertainty. Very rare are the souls who leave their hearth and home and take refuge in God, whose door is always open to them. To such souls, my call is: "Come to your spiritual home. The choice is entirely yours."

Surrender of the ego

Surrender of the ego is the first step towards samarpan. A devotee can only qualify for samarpan if he is able to make a total offering of his ego. Many great, truthful, honest and pure people have missed out because they were unable to empty themselves of ego. So far in history, only very innocent people like Mirabai, Christ, Ramdas, Ramakrishna

Paramahamsa or Ramana Maharshi have obtained the highest state of samarpan.

When one surrenders to divinity, life becomes happy and glorious. The devotee will not care whether there is joy or sorrow, gain or loss, because he has surrendered to the will of the Divine, and whatever He brings into his life is welcome. Samarpan does not mean prostrating before someone; it means surrendering the ego and intellect. This is not an easy process. If there is anything difficult in life, it is surrendering the ego which stands in the way of truth. However, the ego dies when meditation is born. The ego dies when bhakti is in full bloom. The ego dies when awareness becomes overwhelming. The vision of God is born out of the death of the ego. When the ego is surrendered, tensions leave the *jiva*, the individual soul, and cravings for pleasurable experiences dwindle into nothing.

It is the crude ego which is surrendered in the sadhana of samarpan. What one actually surrenders is the limited identity and small self, so that one stops struggling and flows with the current of the Supreme Self. Sorrow is rooted in the limited ego, in the mind and the senses. If this ego can be surrendered at His lotus feet, all one's miseries will come to an end.

Perfect surrender requires the highest level of detachment, *vairagya*. However, what people usually surrender to is the sensory mind and worldly attachments. The mind says, "Do this," and one does it. The mind says, "Say this," and one says it. The mind says, "Desire this," and one desires it. The mind says, "Reject that," and one rejects it. One has become a slave of the mind. The real meaning of surrender is to detach, to renounce worldly existence and attach oneself to the Divine. It means not being a slave to mental whims, fantasies and desires, but transcending the lower mind and communing with the higher Self.

Surrender is not possible if earthly desires remain in the heart of the devotee. God's grace does not descend until there is absolute, selfless projection of the ego. For this to happen, all the dross of the human nature and personality has to be removed. God forever accepts the surrender of a real devotee and in return gives His glory, His power, everything. God is captivated by supreme love, *para bhakti*, by devotion which is intense, totally absorbing and full of deep adoration. The supreme and selfless love of a para bhakta allows him to merge fully and completely with God. Such a devotee has no awareness of his own identity; he has no ego apart from his devotion to God. He no longer even thinks of himself as a devotee. His mind is so absorbed in God that he feels himself as God.

For the para bhakta everything merges into a homogeneous state. He becomes one with God and experiences divinity in everything. When the whole world is perceived as God, no books need to be studied, no meditation needs to be practised, nothing needs to be contemplated, and no hearing, thinking or introspection are required. There is no need to go to a forest, no need to enter a cave and no need to retire to the Himalayas. When everything is God, how can 'I' exist? 'I' does not exist; there is only Him. To attain Him one simply has to merge one's existence with Him, surrender oneself to Him.

External changes

To live in communion with the Divine, one does not have to reject society or renounce action. One does not have to renounce love, service or any good act or intention that brings about purification. Only the weakness in the personality needs to be renounced. The aspirant has to know how to discard all that is unwanted within. This cannot be achieved intellectually; it is only possible by living it in daily life.

Samarpan is not only a mental sadhana. Outer changes also help to attain total surrender to the Divine. What made St Francis of Assisi a saint? It was not his realization of God, Christ or religion, or his compassion and love. Initially, his inspiration was the vow of poverty and chastity that he had taken. To move from a life of luxury to a life of poverty and maintain that discipline is very difficult. One must have the capacity to make external changes, to take a vow and live by it, without giving in to weakness and infirmity.

A vow, *vrat*, reflects a change in lifestyle. One must test oneself and undergo a little physical hardship. Sleep on a mattress on the floor one night a week. Miss a meal one day a week and eat lightly the next day. By making certain adjustments and disciplining oneself little by little, this change in lifestyle will influence the mind. In this way, the practice of surrender comes about. It is moment to moment awareness of living with higher principles, with absolute faith in the higher spirit. One need not bother about one's faults, because every human being has infinite power within. This power needs to be awakened. The weakness of those who aim high is not regarded as weakness, but as their special trait.

Purification of thoughts

The mind of the devotee is the *kalpataru*, the wish-fulfilling tree. When the mind merges in His consciousness, then communion becomes spontaneous and automatic. The feelings arising in this mind are converted into spiritual power. If the sadhaka's mind is full of faith, fearlessness, hope and goodness, he receives infinite boons. Therefore, mental equilibrium is of prime importance for an aspirant. If he becomes frightened in adverse conditions and loses his precious faith, he is lost.

Once a weary traveller decided to rest in the shade of a kalpataru. He was thirsty and wished, "If only I had some water!" At that very moment, some village women were returning home with pots full of water fresh from a well, and they gave him some to drink. Next he wished for a comfortable bed to sleep on. Lo, a cart of straw passed by and as it swayed about on the bumpy road, bales of straw fell out, so he could make a fine bed to sleep on. Now the sun was setting, and as he surveyed the wild forest surrounding him, he became

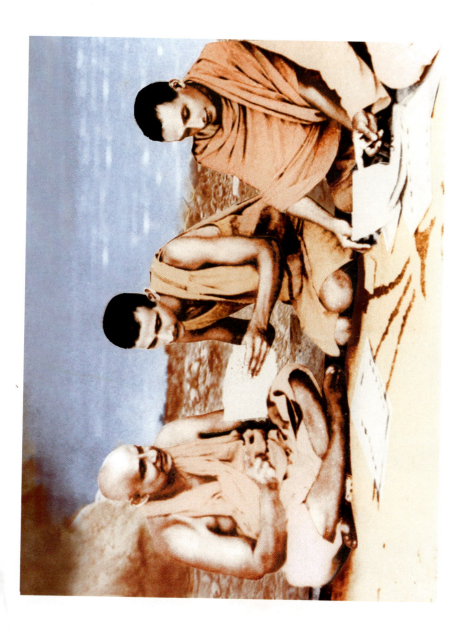

terrified at the thought of being eaten by a tiger. Lo, a tiger leaped out of the bushes and devoured him!

The vital mind, the seat of consciousness, must only have those thoughts that are conducive to one's spiritual progress. All other thoughts will need to be annihilated. As devotion becomes intense, one will have many miraculous experiences. One's thoughts will materialize. If the mind is in tune with name and form, one will be able to receive anything. Nevertheless, one must always be humble and know that *siddhis*, spiritual powers, are obstacles on the path.

Should one acquire any *siddhi*, spiritual power, it should never be used for any worldly purpose, but instead placed in a long-term fixed deposit. One day the accomplishments will pay the richest dividend in the form of perfect knowledge, *atma jnanam*. It is precisely for this reason that the yogic scriptures say that siddhis are a disease. When one emerges from samadhi, siddhis are perceived as attainments, but when in samadhi, they are obstacles to perfect surrender of the mind. Therefore, one should use only one's normal accomplishments in life, not the spiritual ones.

Shedding fear

Another quality the aspirant must be wary of is fear. Cowards never acquire the faith of life. Impressions of fear are obstructions to spiritual progress. One should pray that the fear of this or other worlds, fear of the seen and the unseen, fear of the gross and the subtle, fear of acquisition and loss, fear of gods and demons, fear of life and death, fear of attachment and aversion, all leave. Fear is always an imaginary belief, a hindrance to the personality, and no one is free from its influence. But one should proceed on the spiritual path only if one is ready to fully shed fear, otherwise one may as well retrace his steps. One who is afraid of a fly will never be able to enter the lion's den.

The aspirant must also discard fear of worldly difficulties. He should let go of the ever-changing beliefs and foolish sentiments if he wishes to stay in the imperishable and luminous realms. He should remain unmoved even if stones are hurled at his head, remain steadfast even if the influence of this world or the other suffocates him. He should live like a lotus in mud; be self-absorbed and self-attuned like the shirisha tree. If he really wants to walk this path, where except for the self he will find no shelter, he should tell his samskaras, "Hands off." One whose actions announce that his activities are not for show, with his heart set on surrender, moves forward. One whose heart is blossoming with devotion attains Him without doing anything.

Tapasya

Tapasya, often translated as austerity, is undergoing the process of suffering spontaneously and willingly without any attachment, knowing that if one does not willingly undergo this process, nature will compel one to do so. It is, however, not self-mortification, but an attitude that helps the aspirant to see all trials and tribulations as forms of grace. It allows one to accept them as challenges, to maintain steadiness of mind, intelligence and judgement through thick and thin, and to expel negative karmas smoothly. If the suffering is terrible, then it is all the more necessary to elevate the state of the mind.

Trials serve as a barometer to indicate the subtleness and grossness of the imperfect personality. Without trying conditions, one would be unable to gauge the depth of one's personality. When the scales are heavily loaded against one, consider the situation as a gift from Him. Everything, not only the pleasures and comforts, but also the humiliations and hardships should be considered as His gifts, an expression of His will. It is very important to contemplate this point carefully. Often people tend to look upon suffering as failure. No matter what happens, one should never think that one has failed. If God has given suffering, it means that it was needed. If He has given comfort, that was also needed. Everything one receives in life is destined. Whatever is occurring at any given moment has to be undergone for one has to be able to fill in the time. Sitting idly all day doing nothing will lead to depression. For this reason God has created karma for humanity. Every spiritual aspirant must realize this fact. One must be able to perceive suffering as the will of a great power, and realize that it has a spiritual purpose. This fundamental faith is lacking in people's lives today. The most difficult yoga practice is being able to see His mysterious role in all trials and discomforts. Usually, when losses and failures are experienced, one is full of complaints. Only a tapasvi can live calmly and quietly under any circumstances, for he is placed completely at the disposal of the supreme will.

Praise, appreciation, love and recognition only stand in the way of spiritual progress. Still one continues to crave them. How unfortunate that one is lured by praise and favour, but when trials come, one cries out aloud to Him to help take them away. All that is being taken away are divine chances. Praise may destroy the soul, but abuse, insult, injury and discomfort will strengthen the personality. There is no lotus without mud, no pearl without an oyster. From mistakes purity emerges, for it is all willed by the divine force.

Order in chaos

The aspirant must realize that an individual is only a tiny part of the cosmic or universal process. He is nothing; smaller than a molecule or an atom. He is a tiny cog in that untold universal process. Things are moving along in the history and geography of divinity. He will be tossed this way or that, and if he does not accept it, he will always be unhappy.

Someone must have created the great universe that surrounds us. Beyond the perishable forms there must be someone immortal. God is mysterious. Mysterious are His ways. He sent Gautama Buddha to the forest just to make him wise and preach that such a step was not necessary for nirvana. Infinitely gracious is He. Will one believe? There is no other way, except to let Him do His will. There is no alternative to participating in His un-understandable lila.

Pre-planned divine arrangements and ordinances cannot be written off, because there is no escape from them.

It was the will of God that influenced Kaikeyi and led to Rama's fourteen year exile. What for? The mere mortal plunged in ignorance and delusion cannot make sense of His plans, which may seem whimsical and His orders beyond understanding. However, the true devotee knows that it is always better to dance to unseen tunes and feel happy with all changes and dispositions. Rama did it. One should remember the saying, "Pain is a cross on which nature hangs a man whenever she wishes to make him a sublime superman." Finite mortals do not know and cannot understand His infinite blessings in disguise.

God creates every event with a great purpose behind it. Wise men do not oppose it, for they know His mission. Samskaras of the past and the present have to be fried. Disease, discomforts, disturbances, insults and unpleasant situations all help the aspirant to purge the foreign matter from his ego so that he can see his soul. The aspirant must understand that he works, eats and lives for Him alone. It is He who has created all the seen and unseen worlds. It is all His play and unless one plays His game one will miss the joy of life and continue wallowing in self-pity and worldly misery. This knowledge should sustain one's zeal, aim and faith. Lord Krishna says in the *Srimad Bhagavatam*: "Slowly I snatch his wealth, on whom I bestow my grace. Relations also leave the company of that person. When he attempts to regain his lost wealth, I again deceive him, and being disappointed, he decides to keep company with my devotees. Then I bestow my grace on him without any cause."

God's grace descends in unknown ways. To receive it, the seers say, requires complete faith in God. Let one's faith in God be so deep that one submerges fully in Him, so that sorrow is transformed into happiness. Despair goes and hope comes. Sorrow and pain are like day and night; they come and go, continually changing their positions like a rotating wheel. Hence, every aspirant should look upon all that has been given as part of the cosmic order. One should let the senses function on their plane and keep the mind quiet. One should rise above doubt and indecision. One should let go of the thoughts and practise inner silence. One should be indifferent towards the world and awake to the Supreme Self. That is the best way to fight the negative forces that cloud the personality.

13

Stepping into Samarpan

In the sadhana of samarpan, everything the devotee is attached to is eventually renounced. This is, however, a difficult ideal. While it is not difficult to renounce old clothes or worn out objects, it is very difficult to renounce the person or object one loves. Most of the time people practise convenient renunciation, renouncing objects they dislike. However, renouncing what one likes is real renunciation.

The inability to let go of one's likes is due to *moha*, attachment. Only very rarely is an aspirant able to go beyond moha, and it is almost certainly not possible to overcome it at the beginning of the spiritual journey. In spite of the desire to give up *maya*, attachment and infatuation with the world, the devotee is not able to shake them off due to the *vasanas*, inherent desires. He is not able to overcome them or calm the excitement of the mind, pranas and senses. There are also aspirants who would like to renounce, but whose lifestyle does not allow it. After being used to cars, air-conditioners and attached bathrooms, it is not possible to suddenly retreat to a cave. Therefore, the spiritual aspirant is advised to begin the inner journey by continuing to perform actions, but with a changed inner attitude. Eventually, a point comes when the aspirant seeks happiness, rest and light in the self alone, and then neither desire, infatuation or attachment are obstructions.

Transcend karma through karma

An aspirant on the path of samarpan must understand that renunciation of *karma*, action, duty, is not the way to gain spiritual knowledge. Only by participating in karma is the attachment to karma renounced. Karma is relative and *jnana*, knowledge, is also relative, because they are both experiences of the mind. Any experience one has through the mind is not absolute; it is limited. In order to have absolute experience, one must transcend the mind, and the mind cannot be transcended unless one transcends karma by performing karma.

In the *Yoga Vasishtha*, Sage Vasishtha tells Rama, "You will have to work, become king and rule over your subjects. You will have to administer and create law and order. You will have to do many things, and there is no harm in that. Just remember that everything is an idea. Jnana is an idea and karma is an idea, renunciation is an idea, desire and passion are also ideas. Even spiritual experience is an idea, for the whole world is maya, a conglomeration of ideas."

The cycle of karma is endless. Performing karma with non-attachment is the only means to step off the wheel of karma. If one wants to transcend material life or karma, one will have to go through it, but not like the average individual who is ignorantly entangled in it. One can become an emperor, a general, a swami, an administrator, a housewife, a trader, a businessman, an artist or an engineer. These are all an expression of one's karma. Sage Vasishtha says: "Rama, even though you will rule a kingdom, it does not stand in the way of spiritual life. Renunciation of objects and duties is not renunciation. It is renunciation of the idea or identification that is important. One must fulfil obligations, the duties of nature. Only then will these duties not be in direct confrontation with spiritual life."

If non-attachment can be developed, then one can evolve spiritually as well as fulfil the purpose of nature. Those who aspire for spiritual life or meditate for long hours without fulfilling the purpose of nature do not succeed in their endeavours. If an aspirant gives up all his duties, performs no action and meditates all day in a cave, he will experience darkness, not receive the light. This holds true for the average aspirant, who is not a Milarepa or a Buddha. For one who has not fulfilled the purpose of nature through karma, meditation alone will lead to darkness. This is the central teaching of the Upanishads, the *Bhagavad Gita* and also of *Sanatana dharma*, the eternal vedic values. All say that before enlightenment, the primordial karmas and samskaras must first be eliminated.

Sage Vasishtha ends his instructions to Rama by saying: "Even if the world is unreal, participate, because even that participation is unreal. Even if everything that is happening is stupidity, participate. Be stupid with the stupid and foolish with fools."

Participate in the world with a higher purpose

If one waits for the stage where all connection with the natural functioning of the mind and senses has been given up, one will meet with disappointment. Instead, the flow of sentiments should be diverted towards the light of chidakasha and knowledge of *Brahman*, the ultimate reality. One will have to change the ideals and spiritualize the sentiments, experiences and perceptions.

It is not necessary to kill karma or desire. It is also unnecessary to sever all relationships in order to realize the highest Truth. It is not necessary to suppress aversion. Rather than fighting against these factors, simply try to direct them to the Divine. A time will come when the individual realizes that the stream of vasanas is flowing rapidly towards *mahayajna*, the highest sacrifice. One will have relationships, but only with one's ideals. One will have attachment, but only for one's *ishta*, chosen deity; one will have greed, but only for yogic attainments; any discontent will be due to indolence in sadhana. In this way, without destroying the senses and their functions, one will be able to use them for the mahayajna.

As long the highest stage of vairagya, *para vairagya*, absence of any attachment, is not attained, one's relationships and knowledge of the world should be used solely for spiritual devotion, or else one will lose one's faith and again become like an average human being. Every aspirant will have to reckon with this truth.

One has to know the trick of acquiring non-attachment and spiritualization. One should not be influenced either by thoughts of imagined faults and weaknesses or greatness. On the contrary, one should take frequent flights in chidakasha and meet the Purusha again and again. All activities will then move towards the experience of unity or oneness, even though on the surface the aspirant will appear to be a worldly person. This is the inner trick, which has no connection with the intellect. One can absorb this in a moment or never; it is a matter of understanding.

The aspirant should remain unaffected by extraneous circumstances and think, reflect, live and act like an *avadhoota*, free from all worldly attachments. One may move on the earth, go to new regions, live in gardens, on islands, hear music, acquire perfumes, see the sun and the moon, bathe in the Ganga, Yamuna and Saraswati, listen to celestial music, roam about Mt Kailash, but remain here where one is. These are the instructions the guru gives to the disciple committed to the path of samarpan. If the disciple has accepted the challenge with intensity, devotion, faith and sacrifice, he will definitely be successful.

Everyone has an inner instrument which can prevent the influence of external events affecting the astral body. Some know it by the name of dispassion, *vairagya*, some call it devotion, *bhakti*, but they are one and the same. If the mind liberates itself from attachment to the senses, then know it to be renunciation. When it attaches itself to God, know it to be bhakti. When bhakti comes, the superimposition of the world disappears. If bhakti is strong, the state of samarpan comes effortlessly; this is the only instrument by which the impact of daily existence does not influence the inner being. It is the major condition for the fulfilment of surrender.

All attachment should be abandoned except the longing to realize the Supreme Being, so that ultimately one's life may be surrendered in Him. The rest of life must go on as a mere matter of routine. The necessities of daily life should be fulfilled, but one's restlessness, longing, intense devotion and memory must always be for communion with God. Inertia persists as long as adoration and devotion are absent. Laziness in surrender exists as long as intense devotion for God and longing to realize Him are absent. Therefore, along with dispassion for worldly affairs there should be love for God. The weakness of sadhakas is that they give up attachment for the world and abandon sense objects without first acquiring divine love and divine attachment. The result is that along with dispassion and non-attachment, inactivity envelops them. Therefore, together with non-attachment, one should actively seek realization of one's goal.

Samarpan does not mean escapism; it is a symbol of *tyaga*, renunciation. Surrender does not mean that worldly life should be avoided. On the contrary, it is a state of service to humanity through the awakening of spiritual power. One is totally unattached, acting without ego, doing things simply for the sake of others. The goal of samarpan is the public benefit or the collective good, the use of yogic power for the welfare of other people. The aspirant is a trustee, and gives to others whatever God has put before him. His wealth is no longer used to merely elevate his own level of luxury, comfort and status, but at least a part of it is offered for the welfare of others. When one sees oneself as a trustee, then nothing belongs to one; one is only a caretaker, a manager, an implementer of His plan.

Act without anticipation
The central philosophy of the *Bhagavad Gita* is action without attachment, without physical or emotional involvement, without involvement of the ego. Any action may be performed, but it will not be binding. Karma yoga is a method of surrendering the ego, detaching from the likes and dislikes. The essence of non-attachment and dispassion needs to be understood. Non-attachment is a science, not carelessness or

indifference. In the third chapter of the *Bhagavad Gita*, Arjuna asks Lord Krishna: "Without renunciation, how can I attain realization? If I do not renounce, then I will be attached to the things of the world. Will that not hinder my spiritual progress?" Lord Krishna replies: "One can live life fully. One can interact with every being, object and event in life and experience everything totally, but without attachment."

This is the attitude of a yogi who lives in the world without being affected by it. Two important points need to be remembered. One is karma, action, and the other is the fruit of karma, the result of the action. When one is concerned with karma, not with the results, it is non-attachment or karma yoga, but when one is more concerned with the outcome, it is attachment.

All karmas produce *samskaras*, impressions, but actions performed as karma yoga do not produce any samskaras. Any action performed with selflessness, with total detachment, does not rebound on a person. However, an action performed for the fulfilment of a motive rebounds on the individual again and again. Therefore, one must continue to perform karma, involve oneself in every action, discharge all one's responsibilities as *purushartha*, fulfilment of one's duties, but withdraw both emotionally and mentally from any expectation of results. The motive must be clear: "I am a human being, I have incarnated as a jivatma; therefore I have accumulated karma, *sanchit karma*, and I have to work it out. I have to manifest it. When I manifest my karma through karma yoga, I detach myself from the consequences." It is a very simple philosophy.

Attachment is not related to karma, nor is it related to interactions with other people, events or experiences. Attachment is concerned with the fruits or outcome of karma. Everyone should understand this very important factor. In the course of one's life, every day, one interacts with people and experiences love, hate, happiness and unhappiness. When the experience becomes unpleasant or unsatisfying, one does not know what to do. People think that their wife or husband is the cause of their unhappiness and divorce each other, but that does not solve the problem, because one has given up, not detached oneself. Renunciation of an object or a person is one thing and non-attachment to the fruits of the interaction or relationship is another. In the *Bhagavad Gita* (5:11), Lord Krishna says: "Having renounced attachment, a yogi performs actions through the body, mind, intellect and senses, for self-purification." Then, whatever one does in life becomes yoga.

Realize the nature of the unreal

How can non-attachment be practised? Worldly desires are the very basis of the physical body. Attachment dogs the aspirant like a shadow, and self-realization is far away. Who has the patience to try for it? Non-attachment can only be practised when one realizes the true purpose of existence. When it is understood that one is born not just to live and die, to enjoy things and forget them, but for a greater purpose, then the aspirant will begin to discover his real nature. The state being experienced now is physical, mental and emotional, not spiritual. When a person realizes that he is born in order to grow spiritually, to know his true nature, to experience things beyond time, space and matter, then his life, even as a householder, takes on a different meaning.

One is born, one grows up, one is educated, one gets married, has a family and a job. As long as everything goes smoothly, a person remains immersed in ignorance, but if he suddenly gets a knock, a jolt or shock, such as losing his wife, his business, his friends or falling seriously ill, then comes a realization. He looks around and begins to see what life really is. At this point discrimination and non-attachment start to develop. Sometimes one becomes neurotic, thinking about the same thing for days and months on end. Finally one says, "For how long am I going to think?" At that point, one is trying to withdraw from that obsessive thought. That is detachment.

Seeds of unhappiness are concealed in the happiness obtained from the world. Searching for happiness in this body is the cause of disease, old age and death. Happiness derived from power or position becomes coveted due to ignorance. Happiness obtained through attachment results only in unhappiness. But all appearances of happiness are consumed in the fire of dispassion, and when this happens, the experience of bliss that is derived is real and lasting. This bliss, however, is hidden.

To obtain the hidden bliss, one must resort to truth, not to the body and mind. It must be realized that all sentiments are self-created, each worldly relationship is perishable, every thought is changing, limited and finite, every belief is a creation of the mind. It is important to realize this in order to awaken the desire for non-attachment and progress in sadhana. One must change the ideals, sentiments and aspirations, transform one's speech, perceptions and conduct, alter the conduct of one's life. The senses must be turned inwards, the mind quietened and distractions stopped; one must be steady and immovable like the Buddha. One must ask: Who am I? Where am I? Why do I exist?

In *Yoga Vasishtha*, Sage Vasishtha explains to Rama the notions of time, space, object, idea, imagination, emotion and their relationship to spiritual progress and also to bondage. How does desire bind a person and how does it also make him free? How do love and hate bind one and how do they make one free? In this context, Sage Vasishtha narrates a story about a king and his queen, Lilawati.

One day the king and the queen were discussing politics and family affairs. The queen was sleepy and dozed off. She had a dream in which she became old and died. She was reborn, became a child, became a young woman, married, had children, became old again and died. Seven times she was reborn, went through a lifetime and died. Then she woke up. Barely two minutes had passed and the king was still talking.

In that short time she had the experience of seven lives. It was just as real to her as her waking state, for in her dream she enjoyed childhood and youth, loved her different husbands and children, and also suffered in old age. Everything was real in the dream from the point of view of experience. Of course, when her level of consciousness returned to the wakeful state, the experiences had no relevance, but nevertheless she had undergone them.

In the same way, if one changes the level of awareness, then the mental and emotional situations being confronted now will be as irrelevant as the dream experiences of Lilawati. When Lilawati was undergoing the dream experiences, they were real for her. However, when she changed her level of mind, only then did they become relative.

Sage Vasishtha explains to Rama that there is not one, but many levels of experience. In each level, the experiences one has appear to be real, but when one transcends that level, those experiences have no validity. A seemingly valid and real experience is one that the mind identifies with, nothing more.

The question arises then as to why our soul is deluded and ignorant. Why has the individual forgotten his real nature? Why and when did this delusion cover the soul? No one has given a proper answer. All the vedas and scriptures are silent on this point. It can simply be said that the Lord Himself is playing a wonderful game.

When the consciousness is plugged into the world and its objects, one is affected and consequently sorrow and joy are experienced and one become a victim of the positive and negative charges of nature. An insult will affect a person because the senses are receptive to the spoken word, but once he is asleep he will not be affected by any insult. Ignorance is rooted in the mind and the senses. If the mind can be managed, or surrendered to His feet, one's miseries will come to an end. As long as one is unaware of the great power of cosmic consciousness, universal consciousness, divine consciousness, sorrows and miseries cannot be removed.

If the shell of a fresh coconut is broken, the inner kernel will also be broken, but if the coconut is dry, the inner part will remain unaffected because the kernel has detached itself from the shell. Similarly, if the soul is not identified with the body, one will not be affected by what happens to the body. One needs to experience and know that the soul is distinct from the body, from the subtle and the gross body. An individual has to detach and discover the soul lying dormant in the folds of prakriti.

In order to know the higher Self, a true awareness of reality has to be developed, which is neither mental nor intellectual. That deeper awareness develops only through spiritual illumination, which continues to intensify with the gradual removal of impurities. The impurity of the mind is destroyed through the practice of yoga; through the vast range of disciplines such as yama, niyama, asana, pranayama, pratyahara, dharana, dhyana and samadhi, etc.

With awareness of reality, ignorance and prakriti both disappear. There are different types of knowledge, such as that acquired through the sensory organs, through the intellect or reasoning, through personal contact, hearing, imagination and past memories. However, if one wants to realize the nature of the Supreme, knowledge from these sources cannot be depended upon. A different source of knowledge is needed, known as discriminative awareness, *viveka khyati*.

As discriminative awareness develops, it takes the consciousness through different stages of contemplative experiences. First, what is to be avoided; second, awareness of the means of removal; third, awareness of spiritual evolution; fourth, awareness of fulfilment and accomplishment; fifth, awareness of the purpose of experience and liberation; sixth, awareness of the fulfilment of the work of the gunas; and lastly, awareness of reality, and one's own Self.

Raise the consciousness
To practise non-attachment within the framework of household life, an aspirant must first raise the level of his consciousness and mind, develop his philosophy and then try to detach from the karma he is involved in. Otherwise, if

he tries to practise non-attachment just by reading the *Bhagavad Gita*, it will lead to chaos in the family.

Cultivating positive virtues, *maitreyi bhava,* is the first aspect of raising the quality of mind. The aspirant feels positive about everyone and everything, without envy, jealousy, greed or possessiveness, which develops good mental patterns that will help overcome the obstacles of procrastination, depression or laziness. The mind will then be purified, allowing the consciousness to rise. If someone is happy, one should feel good, and if someone is suffering, the positive response is to feel compassion. If one is being criticized, feel thankful that a fault is being pointed out, which one might otherwise have been unaware of. The world becomes a mirror and gives everything the aspirant needs to move in the desired direction.

The aspirant also needs to cultivate contentment of the highest order, for without it there is no possibility of holding the mind in a state of equilibrium. The sadhaka has to establish a state of constant equilibrium and stillness by a deliberate and powerful resolve, sankalpa, meditation, and any other means available. He aims at attaining a state of perfect calm and serenity, whatever happens in the external or internal environment. The aim is not merely to acquire the ability to quell a mental disturbance when it arises, but the more rare power to prevent any disturbance from taking place at all. Once a disturbance has been allowed to occur, it takes far more energy to overcome it completely. Even if outwardly it disappears quickly, the inner subconscious disturbance persists for a long time.

To reach such a state of equanimity, the aspirant needs to develop an extremely positive and dynamic condition of mind, which has nothing in common with a negative mentality based on laziness and lack of initiative. It is based on perfect indifference to all personal enjoyment, comfort and other considerations that sway humanity. Its object is attainment of that peace which takes one completely beyond the realm of illusion, misery and entanglement in worldly life.

The state of supreme contentment and non-attachment cannot be acquired by mere assertion of the will. It is the result of prolonged self-discipline and undergoing much pain and suffering. Habit is stronger than nature, and habits developed through innumerable lifetimes cannot be changed all at once. Constant alertness and training of the mind to maintain the right attitude of viveka and vairagya is necessary.

Let experience become philosophy

When trying to raise his consciousness, the aspirant is also trying to develop a philosophy to live by. However, this is not a philosophy derived from the intellect, but one based on direct experience, *aparokshanubhuti*. Non-attachment cannot be developed by thinking, or through any other intellectual process. Intellectually, the individual may know that nothing belongs to him and that everything is temporary. He may say it every day, but as there is so much 'mineness' and attachment, whatever happens to someone else affects him too, since he relates to the events. In order to practise non-attachment, therefore, one has to develop a philosophy through which one can have a different relationship with everything. However, to have that philosophy one must have an experience which changes the quality of the mind, otherwise non-attachment cannot be understood. To understand anasakti, vairagya, sannyasa or non-attachment, one must have an altered quality of mind, which has come about through experience.

A sadhu and an ordinary man were neighbours. One day the sadhu heard his neighbour crying because his goat had died. The sadhu told him, "Sooner or later everything has to die." He explained that crying would not bring the goat back and was able to pacify his friend. Three months later, the sadhu's cow died. He became so miserable that he stayed secluded in his hut in a deep depression. Remembering how he had been consoled by the sadhu's wise words, his neighbour said, "What if your cow is dead? Everything has to die." The sadhu interrupted, "Go away. I don't want to hear your words of wisdom." The man replied, "But when my goat died, you consoled me with the same wisdom." The mahatma became angry and shouted, "That was all right for your goat, but this is my cow."

What the sadhu experienced, every individual experiences every day of his life. When the sadhu was imparting wisdom to his neighbour, he had a certain quality of mind which he could not maintain when his own cow died, because his philosophy was based on the intellect, not on experience.

One may read the whole of *Yoga Vasishtha*, but if an accident takes place in one's family, one will definitely be affected, for the teachings have only enlarged the scope of the intellect, not brought about a fundamental transformation in the structure of awareness. One may say, "Life is transient," but the tranquillity goes when disaster strikes. A transformation in the realm of awareness, aparokshanubhuti or direct experience, is required. It can be brought about by the practice of dhyana yoga, self-introspection, mantra, etc., along with the practices of karma yoga and bhakti yoga.

Be thou a yogi
Yoga is a science of life. It is not an act of renunciation, not escapism, not negation or rejection of life, but correcting the wrong notions and impressions formed over lifetimes. In the *Bhagavad Gita* (18:1–5) Arjuna says to Lord Krishna: "I desire to know the essence or truth of sannyasa. Is it tyaga? Is it renunciation?" Lord Krishna replies: "Some sages say renounce all action with desire, and others say renounce only the fruits of action. Some philosophers declare that action should be abandoned, while others say that acts of helping others, giving to others and purification should not be renounced. My conclusion is that renunciation is of three kinds: sattwic, rajasic and tamasic. Anything that is good, sattwic or auspicious should not be renounced. *Yajna*, sacrifice for the benefit of others, *daan*, giving to others, and *tapas*, purification of body and mind, are not to be surrendered, even by a sannyasin."

One has to renounce the frailties in one's personality. This is only possible by living a yogic life. One must say, "I am a yogi." One must feel it every day. One must not be afraid. In this way, the practice of surrender, the moment to moment awareness of living with higher principles, with absolute faith in the higher spirit, will come about. While the ultimate purpose of yoga is enlightenment, the preliminary purpose is to clean the road, to light the path and make the journey itself.

14

Power of Faith

In the *Bhagavad Gita* (4:39), Lord Krishna says: "One who is full of faith, who is devoted to it, and who has subdued all the senses, obtains knowledge of the Self and, having obtained this knowledge, he at once attains supreme peace, *moksha*, eternal salvation." One may experience *vairagya*, dispassion, one may believe in a higher reality, one may practise a range of sadhanas, but unless one develops a faith so strong that it does not tremble in the face of any storm whatsoever, one's surrender will remain conditional and not culminate into samarpan.

Just as everyone has a spark of divinity, everyone has faith within. This faith needs to be exploded and developed. It is a gradual process, which begins with the guru and ends with the revelation that all is God. Faith cannot be seen, but everyone can feel it. It is a feeling, and it exists just as anger or hate exist and influence the physical functions of the body. The effect of *bhavana*, inner feeling, on the human body is tangible. Therefore, although faith cannot be seen, the effects can be felt on the body. The cause can be known through the effect.

Faith is not merely a belief, it is confidence. Faith is a strong, resolute conviction in the existence of God, in the authority of the revealed scriptures and in the truth of the guru's teachings. It is much deeper than thought; it is an expression of the inner spirit. As one progresses along the path of evolution and leaves behind a trail of emotions, sentiments, memories, sense objects and so on, there is a peak of experience where things which come within a certain range of the mind appear to be a reality. That experience is the basis of faith.

To progress in spiritual life, all that needs to be cultivated is faith. Faith is itself the source of every blessing, every benediction. A good husband or wife, a nice house and plenty of riches can create problems and give rise to doubt. Faith is not a result of external observances; it comes with constant inner awareness, not of the senses or the turbulence and disturbances of the mind, but of the soul, the Atma. As the aspirant goes deeper within and faces the inner light, he becomes faithful. Where there is faith, there is power and enlightenment. Faith can move mountains, part the ocean or dry up the sea.

Faith is indeed the greatest power. Without faith, one may as well forget about *samarpan*, self-surrender. It is no use talking about God because He cannot be surrendered to or realized through mere discussion. One can talk about God for years and eons, but nothing will be achieved. Ramakrishna Paramahamsa used to say that one can keep writing the words 'water, water, water' on a piece of paper, but unless the paper is soaked in water, it will not give water. One needs to soak oneself in faith to surrender to God.

The role of faith

The main purpose of faith and trust is to develop love for God, *bhakti*, even while living in the external, transient world. One does not develop these spiritual attributes merely to solve one's problems, but to develop an experience of God, to have darshan and merge in Him. This should be the aim; if not today, then tomorrow; if not tomorrow, then in the next life.

Faith in God is the first rung on the ladder of spirituality. It inspires hope in the seeker of truth to attain divine grace. Faith allows an aspirant to have perfect trust in God, to abandon all fears, cares, worries and to be at perfect ease.

Faith alone opens the door to eternal bliss and the immortal abode, because faith transcends reason and intellect. One must have unswerving, unshakeable faith to enter the domain of everlasting peace.

The presence of faith makes the disciple aware of the deeper and greater aspects of inner existence. Nothing in the world is difficult for one who has faith. If one has faith in one's guru, one's mantra or one's sadhana, it will work immediately. If faith is properly directed, one can heal sickness, transfer magnetic power, and even move an object through the power of thought.

Faith is a glorious, wish-fulfilling jewel. If one's heart is full of the light of faith, then one's mind and heart will always be radiant. Throughout the day and night there will be no darkness. This illumination does not depend on an external light. Faith dispels the overpowering gloom of ignorance like sunlight dispels clouds. Vanity and ignorance automatically disappear when one possesses the gem of faith. Illumination arises from within, just as the sun rises and removes the darkness.

Propensities like passion, anger and greed will never come near if that gem resides in one's heart. Poison is transformed into nectar and enemies become friends. Those who are suffering mentally will find that their pain disappears. When the jewel of faith in God abides in one's heart, there is no suffering, even in dreams. Therefore, those who strive for that jewel are the wisest.

The devotee will discover that faith brings spontaneity into his life. Even if one does not want to love God, one will love Him. Even if one does not want to surrender, one will have to. Even if one does not want anything from Him, He will give everything. Faith in God brings spontaneous blessings. God also wants spontaneity in His relationship with the devotee. When He gives pain, one must accept it, and not say it is due to a curse or bad karma. People usually think that only good things are God's blessings, but faith turns suffering into a blessing.

God says, "Love for the world and worldly objects should not come in My way. I do not like to appear in a mind where there is dual love and incomplete surrender. The soul that has offered his soul at the altar of my awareness, unto Him I am given." If only one can perfect faith and surrender totally to Him, one can work miracles. Intensity of faith and surrender, unmindful of failures, is the only condition that will allow one's soul to commune with the Divine. God-realization is an outcome of intense, unflinching and non-dual faith. To experience the Divine, one must have faith and belief. There is no other way to attain it.

Faith versus intellect
Faith is a spiritual substance and the main factor behind human existence. If innocent faith could be maintained without any intellectual pollution, one could do anything in life. Knowledge of God is one aspect and faith in God is another. Through knowledge alone one may or may not develop communion; it is never a certainty. Knowledge of God does not necessarily bring one closer or guarantee communion with Him, but faith does. Faith has to be experienced. A child has faith, a disciple has faith, and that faith is realization.

Faith does not demand any proof or epistemological conclusions. One cannot say that one will have faith in God only when one has seen Him. He cannot be seen until one's faith is complete. Faith is an intuitive attitude, which one cultivates inwardly even before coming across an object or a person. It is the first and foremost condition. Of course, faith presupposes love. Thus one loves the object of one's faith. Awareness follows, then surrender, then merging, and finally realization. This is how the aspirant progresses.

There are many stories about saints, miracle workers and great devotees. Things have happened to them and around them which cannot be explained in terms of human knowledge. This is due to faith. One has to guard and protect one's faith, because intellect and logic kill faith. However, if the difference between faith and intellect is understood properly, both can develop simultaneously in their respective directions.

Usually one's faith in God is intellectual. It is therefore not faith at all, but an idea. Most people believe in God; they love, respect and worship Him. That is belief. Generally, when people refer to faith in guru or God, they mean that they are intellectually convinced of the guru's or God's superiority, a notion acquired from their parents or society. What most people have is belief, and it is mistaken for faith. Many also kill the little belief with which they could have survived on the psycho-emotional level. They say there is no God and conduct arguments on the subject, damaging their only link with the divine forces. Therefore, it is necessary to protect one's faith as well as one's belief.

Faith, however, is more than belief. It is a higher energy in a concentrated form. Belief can fail, and sometimes does. Intellect fails, but faith is infallible; it will never fail, because faith is not an expression of the mind. It is understood through the mind, but not expressed through the mind. It has a different source and a different channel.

A human being has intelligence and faith. It is through intelligence that he learns about God, but it is through faith that he experiences God. Not knowledge, but experience comes about through faith. Just as love, enmity, jealousy, joy and sorrow are not the stuff of the intellect but of experience, faith is also a matter of experience. The basis of the intellect is analysis. The Upanishads may have been written with the help of intelligence, but faith is such a substance that it accepts even the invisible. After all, no one has seen anger, but anger exists. This is a matter of faith.

Faith needs to be experienced, not seen. Therefore, at the very beginning of the *Ramacharitamanas*, it has been said, "Without *shraddha* and *vishwas*, faith and deep conviction, even great siddhas cannot achieve spiritual attainment." Even a *siddha*, a spiritually accomplished person, cannot see the God within if he does not have faith and belief.

Faith and belief are essential, though intellect has its own place. Intellectuals ask why idols of gods and goddesses are worshipped. At the level of intellect, this may seem strange. After all, how can a piece of stone be God? How can a piece of paper be God? How can a person who eats and sleeps be guru and God? The intellect may question this, but when it comes to faith, then a stone is indeed God, a leaf is God and a tree is God.

How to find faith

People suffer because of their desires, for there is no end to desires and they will never be fulfilled. Desires are like the waves of the ocean which arise incessantly, one after another. When suffering becomes unbearable and there is no way out, people turn to God. Intense faith develops and then the crisis slowly goes away. But it is when one is in the middle of the crisis that one should transform one's entire life totally. When a situation occurs in which God is experienced as the helper, then and there the aspirant should transform his life and give it a totally new direction. He should leave everything, surrender everything to God, and tread the path to God. Many people experience their prayers being answered, but still they do not see the depth of their own faith.

To develop faith, in the beginning effort is necessary. One has to keep one's inner awareness of faith awake continuously, whether talking, meeting, arguing or explaining something to someone. If this objective is forgotten a few times in the beginning, there should be no frustration. The effort must be persistent. One must try to understand what one is doing. In order to keep the spiritual awareness awake one must be forever alert, optimistic and self-assured. One should have faith in the name and power of one's *ishta*, chosen deity. One must have confidence and conviction in the reality of one's inner essence; only then will this spiritual power work. However, it is quite certain that in the beginning a determined effort must be made. One must be full of determination. "It must and it shall happen" should be the mantra.

When one takes the path of the spirit, that other element begins to rouse. One should now refer to that other element and not look upon oneself as a physical body. What is there in the world that one cannot accomplish? One should let go of doubts, let go of the intellectual question, "What if it does not happen?" Instead revel in the greatness that exists within. Each form of behaviour, each principle, each habit that undermines one's faith should be carefully extracted and removed. One should change one's manner of speaking, ambitions, language and viewpoint. One should change one's self-created convictions and thoughts. Only then will the power of faith be seen manifesting in the depths of one's life.

Any individual who searches for Him with love finds the jewel. Firm faith in God is the reward of all spiritual effort. Whether one practises asana, pranayama, kundalini yoga, raja yoga or rebirthing, the reward has to be faith. However, nobody has ever acquired the jewel of faith without the help of saints. No matter what sadhana one does, ultimately one has to come to a saint. Whosoever bears this in mind and communes with the good finds devotion to God an easy attainment. It is the saints who bring this wisdom to the world.

The term often used for the company of sages is satsang. *Satsang* means association with truth, from *sat*, meaning 'truth', and *sanga*, meaning 'association'. Tulsidas says in the *Ramacharitamanas*:

> *Without satsang, no story of Rama is possible,*
> *And without that there can be no destruction of delusion.*
> *Without the destruction of delusion*
> *No strong devotion to the feet of Rama is possible.*

In order to protect faith, to increase and experience it more fully and intimately, the relationship between God and devotee, or guru and disciple, comes first. This relationship is a matter of total faith, living faith. One has to believe in the same way one believes in one's mother. How does one know that one's mother is really one's mother? Through faith. There has to be the same faith in God and guru.

Milarepa's faith

The story of Milarepa, the great yogi of Tibet, is a story of faith perfected. It is a great revelation for all seekers. Once a young boy was searching for his guru. One day he came across a married lama, who had several disciples. As the boy approached, the guru demanded, "Why have you come here?" "I have come to receive initiation," the boy replied. The guru went inside his house, leaving the boy on the doorstep to ponder why he had really come. Much later, he opened the door and called out, "Who is there?" "It is me," the boy replied, "and I have come to receive the spiritual teachings."

"What, you are still here!" the guru exclaimed and gave him a mighty kick. "Get out of here," he shouted, "I don't want to see you again." The boy said, "But I have come for initiation." The guru said, "No, you are fit for nothing." He abused him in many ways, but the boy did not leave because he was prepared. He had prepared his ego to be attacked, pruned and disintegrated.

Even after Milarepa had been accepted as a disciple, the situation did not improve, but grew worse. Whenever Milarepa asked for the teachings, he received rebukes and abuse. The guru would not allow him to take his place with the other disciples during any initiation or important event, but made him stay alone outside.

When the guru had finished his meals, he would keep the leftovers in the cupboard for two or three days and when it was dry and hard, he would give it to Milarepa. The guru's wife took pity on the boy, and often she would bring him some fresh milk to drink. One day the guru saw Milarepa drinking milk and shouted in rage, "You ungrateful fellow! Now I have caught you stealing my milk! You are unfit to stay in my house any longer." "But where can I go?" Milarepa asked. "Up the mountain," the guru replied. "You can carry stones and build me a house." The boy climbed up the steep mountain and began his arduous sadhana. Every day he carried stones up the mountain, one by one, working from dawn to dusk, until his whole body was bruised and aching, and he could not hoist another stone on to his back.

One day the guru came to inspect the work and saw Milarepa collapsed in exhaustion after carrying a huge boulder from the other side of the mountain. "So this is how you spend your time, you lazy good-for-nothing!" he shouted at him. "Why are you building here when I told you to build further up the mountain? You can't even follow simple instructions, and you want me to give you the sacred teachings!" Milarepa had to dismantle the whole house, stone by stone, carry it further up the mountain and start again. This happened seven times over.

Each time the house was built, the guru appeared and told him to pull it down and build it in a different way. In spite of all the hardships, pain and anguish imposed by the guru, Milarepa never lost his faith. He had unflinching, unshakeable faith in the guru, regardless of his apparent cruelty and hard-heartedness. And Milarepa attained the ultimate in life, transcendental consciousness.

15

Follow the Higher Will

God's will or divine will is a universal reality. It is the most powerful force that conducts each and every activity, seen as well as unseen. When the *jiva*, the individual soul, is attracted by *maya*, the illusory world, he is led far from the divine will and becomes weak, full of fear and anxiety. Once he transcends the barriers of the mind, however, he begins to realize the will of God, which is the destiny of all creation. Once he knows the will of God, he knows how to act and how to manage his life. He becomes aware that he derives strength, inspiration and force from a higher source. This awareness leads to true contentment, and all the faculties become integrated. The faculties of the body merge with those of the mind, those of the mind merge with those of the spirit, and one becomes complete. When this completeness is experienced, the individual sensitivities, attitudes and actions change. Surrender blossoms spontaneously.

A great poet and bhakta has written:

> *All is Thy will.*
> *Thy will be done.*
> *Whether You raise me*
> *To the height of spiritual glory,*
> *Or You throw me down*
> *Into the abyss of hell,*
> *I accept it,*

> *Readily, happily, with pleasure,*
> *For that is Thy will.*
> *I am the chariot,*
> *You are the charioteer.*
> *I am the horse,*
> *You are the master*
> *Keep me as You like.*
> *Use me, misuse me or abuse me,*
> *I have nothing to defend.*

He is the guide

God is always there inside one, beside one and everywhere else. He is the eternal companion. He is there to guide one. Nothing can touch the aspirant who surrenders to His will, who dedicates his actions to Him. Let Him do as He wants, and accept His arrangements as divine grace. God looks after whoever is aware of Him. If the aspirant looks at Him merely through the physical eyes, he will see only as much as those eyes can see. If he thinks of Him merely with his mind, he will think only as much as the mind can think. For eyes see forms and the mind perceives thoughts. Who, then, realizes Him? One who surrenders his sight, his mind and his awareness to Him.

No one has realized God through the physical eyes. He cannot be seen as long as one is watching the rest of the world. The divine music cannot be heard as long as one is concerned with worldly tumults. Only after the external perceptions have been withdrawn and the last traces of lower love and passions have been surrendered, does He come, sing, love and make one into a blessed being. There is no need to think of what might happen afterwards and how; He will do as He deems fit. He may give the power of healing or the power of omniscience. However, this is not the devotee's concern at all. He should not trouble himself with results. Surrender alone is his concern. He must have faith, empty himself and surrender his mind. The rest may be left to the Supreme Guide, to the strange mendicant who protects him at every step of the way.

The devotee who remains aware of his aspiration for samarpan at every stage of his life and sadhana is constantly assisted in his spiritual progress. An aspirant not only needs devotion, but to know he is assisted. Therefore, he should ask himself who assists him when he feels inspired? Who directs his life into sadhana? God takes care of the devotee due to his intense devotion. Reflect upon this carefully.

The will of the Lord reigns supreme; it operates through every individual, every creature, every object. It is possible that even if the aspirant practises nothing, he will find that in three months God has taught him everything, for He is the greatest of all teachers. God may give him everything without anything having been asked of Him. He knows what one needs and deserves. All desires must be discarded and everything surrendered to the divine will. Whether in pain or happiness, one is in His hands. God is the shepherd. One who surrenders to Him will be taken care of. In the Bible, Psalm 23 expresses confidence in God's protection.

The Lord is my shepherd; I shall not want.
He makes me down to lie in pastures green,
and he leads me beside the still waters.
He restores my soul, and He leads me in the paths of righteousness
for His own name's sake.
Yea, though I walk through the valley of the shadow of death,
I shall fear no evil, for He is with me;
His rod and staff comfort me.
He prepares a table before me in the presence of my enemies;
He anoints my head with oil; and my cup overflows.
Surely goodness and mercy will follow me all the days of my life;
And I will dwell in the house of the Lord forever.

Leave it to Him

Allowing oneself to be the recipient of the divine will is the highest virtue that can be cultivated. This is the attitude of total dedication. Ultimately, one has to do nothing except surrender to God's will. Actions lose the strings of attachment once all idea of doership is renounced. Usually the individual identifies with every act and experiences every thought, emotion and feeling that manifests. The attitude is: *Aham karta, aham bhokta* – "I am the doer, I am the enjoyer." However, in order to recognize the will of God, this attitude has to change to: *Naham karta, naham bhokta* – "I am not the doer, I am not the enjoyer." The world will go on as it should. Let life happen, if it happens and as it happens without worrying about anything. Just act as His instrument. Events take their predestined course automatically. It is always safe to surrender the egoistic spirit. One simply has to cooperate in the plan.

One's duty is to work for Him and to be free of affectations. Let Him do the rest, because He knows. The individual should stop, for he knows not. God does everything for one's good, so whatever happens will always be right. His will alone will prevail. Why bother about house repairs when the landlord is already there to do it? This is His temple; let him do as He likes. Surrender will have to be backed up by this attitude. Not for a moment should one forget the fact that He alone looks after all one's needs.

Time should not be wasted going from place to place in a quest to find the greatest guru. The aspirant should continue his spiritual practices and march ahead with faith and humility. He may visit ashrams or other such places with spiritual vibrations from time to time and try to live as quietly as possible, without worrying about the vacuum in his life. He should live in the will of God, for God is first and last. Ultimately, His will comes true. One can do nothing; one is only an instrument.

Ramakrishna Paramahamsa used to tell this story. God laughs on two occasions. He laughs when two brothers divide land between them, place a string across it, and say to each other, "This side is mine and that side is yours." God laughs and says to Himself, "Why, this whole universe is Mine; and about a little clod of earth they say, 'This side is mine and that side is yours'!" God laughs again when the physician says to the mother, weeping bitterly because her child is desperately ill, "Don't be afraid. I shall cure your child." The physician is unaware that no one can save the child if God wills otherwise.

One hundred percent surrender

In order to become an instrument of the divine will, one has to become completely empty. One has to change oneself completely. The attitude should be: "Whatever happens, let it happen. Even if I have cancer, I will accept it." If the devotee has to make a choice between grace and health, his choice is grace.

The aspirant should not just imagine that he is surrendering; he must know how to surrender. Mere prostration is not surrender. He has to be truly able to say, "Thy will be done." He should consecrate himself not only in thought and word, not merely with material possessions, but without any reservations whatsoever. God may have placed him in the best of circumstances, but he must ask himself how he would feel if he lost it all. Will he say, "God, I surrender, but please give me my money and my child."

Most things said about God are just intellectual gymnastics. One may have read a hundred books and be able to quote impressive verses, but the mind is not impressed. People say, "My Lord, I am always dying for you. Thy will be done, but please bring back my husband." What is this business of trying to surrender everything to Him, but keeping a straw for oneself, and then suffering because of that straw? If there is complete surrender to God, nothing is impossible, but the aspirant should not put conditions on the act of surrender. He cannot say, "I worship you, so look after me." God is omniscient; He controls one's mind, prana, life and death. Is He so foolish that He needs to be told to remove one's sorrows? He has given sorrow, joy, wealth, poverty and illness. He knows everything; He is all-powerful, all-pervading. In principle, people accept this, yet they doubt Him. If one truly believed that He is omnipresent, omniscient and omnipotent, one would feel no need to ask Him for anything. One would leave it up to Him.

The art of surrender is a virtue in itself. It must be complete; it must be one hundred percent. The aspirant must go to Him completely naked and empty. Half-hearted surrender is not surrender. Verbal surrender is not surrender. Surrender is born of love; it is abiding and real. Therefore, one should first develop love for Him. Divine love is realized through the grace of God and the blessings of saints, through selfless service and absorbing contemplation and meditation. It is better to be born as a dog or a monkey than a human being who leaves the world without surrendering his little self, his ego. There is no difference between such a person and an animal; both live by instinct.

Try to practise surrender at every moment. It might be impossible to be one hundred percent true to one's convictions at all times, but still one should try. The trials will come, and at that time also one must try one's best to practise acceptance of His will at every moment. After all, a master has to test his servant, to see whether this chap is honest or a hypocrite. He may only be making a show of his bhakti by praying, "I am Thine, my Lord; Thy will be done."

A devotee may go to temples and discharge all the religious obligations as taught by his chosen tradition, but that alone will not help him to unlock the secret inner chambers. At best, it will maintain a psychological sense of fulfilment. However much he may sit for pooja, lack of awareness will render his efforts futile. The name of one's chosen deity may be repeated in any way one likes, anywhere one likes and whenever one likes. However, it must be done with *bhava*, intense awareness, and non-dual faith. There must be complete surrender to one's sadhana. No effort should be spared, caring neither for success nor failure. Mental equilibrium must be maintained by remaining a witness. The aspirant is working according to His orders. He will give one the necessary inspiration and provide suitable opportunities to render the divine work successful.

One has to go in, so that where there are now two, there will be only one. There should be complete identification, fullness of sentiment and experience of proximity. Then there will be union of the formless, *nirakara,* and the one with form, *sakara.* This is the state of samarpan.

Become an instrument

The devotee must practise thinking that the individual self is not real, it does not exist, but what is real is the power that works through the individual in all things. Eventually, practice will reveal this secret. Day and night it must be remembered: "He resides unseen within me and He makes me perform all actions." One must contemplate this and realize its meaning. When it is firmly rooted in the mind, then every act will be one of surrender. One must realize, through experience, that He is making one do everything. One should, through awareness, stay away from the belief that one is the doer. In this manner, one will gradually come to realize the knowledge of the doer. One has to efface oneself; one has to awaken Him. First one must know Him to be the doer in all ordinary matters, for which detachment, dispassion and discrimination will need to be developed. Slowly, as this practice matures, one will be convinced that one is also the same entity.

In order to become an instrument, it is necessary to practise one's convictions. One must resolve to remove *ajnana,* ignorance, and believe oneself to be a child of God. Just as an infant learning to walk moves forward step by step towards the outstretched hands of his parents, so too shall one move forward step by step and in complete surrender. One must resolve not to allow any problem, great or small, to stand in the way. For a sincere aspirant, the most important thing is to empty himself. The Divine cannot enter one who is not empty, who is full his own desires, choices, difficulties and problems. A disciple need not be an idiot. He may be very intelligent, very funny, very capable, but before God he is nothing.

There are many stories of disciples who attempted to be mediums, but failed. Swami Sivananda had many disciples, most of whom were outstanding people. However, only those who completely surrendered to him became his mediums. When one becomes the medium of God or guru, one does not choose what to become. His wish is done through one. To begin with, therefore, one should drop one's choices.

A disciple has to learn many things in order to become a good medium or conductor. The five *kleshas*, or afflictions, must be removed. This is the mental sattwic state. The bowels must be kept clean. This is the physical sattwic state. Relationships must be conducted along appropriate lines. This is the emotional sattwic state. The disciple must let God think through him and work through him. If he is able to surrender to Him, He will make the disciple His medium. This is the psychic sattwic state.

Within every individual there exist many cosmic worlds and many gods, not on the plane of external consciousness, but on another plane. These cosmic worlds are nothing other than symbols of the areas of consciousness. As the mind becomes subtler and subtler, one has visions of such cosmic worlds or penetrates into the realms of spiritual consciousness. When the mind is totally dedicated and surrenders itself, currents flow from the mind itself. The intellect is an obstruction here, and faith is the aid. When all the contents of the mind are exhausted, everything becomes easy. After the mind, the unconscious is exhausted, and then the Self merges with the universal consciousness, the divine consciousness.

In order to experience this, the path is meditation. At least two hours a day should be devoted to meditation practice. An aspirant may begin with ten minutes of meditation practice and gradually build up to two hours. In ten minutes, nothing happens. It takes at least fifteen minutes for the disturbances of the body to settle down. It takes almost half an hour for the brain to settle down. For another half an hour one has to fight with the mind, and after one and a half hours the mind sleeps. Meditation is a threefold process: the meditator, the object of meditation and the process of meditation. Throughout the practice, there is awareness of these three things, but this must drop, which means becoming empty. One should not be afraid of this emptiness. When one becomes empty, there is nothing to block the flow of divine energy. It can flow through one's mind, through one's intuition, through one's speech, through one's palms. In some people the energy flows through their eyes. Mahatma Gandhi was such a person. When he looked into someone's eyes, that person was under his control.

'Thy will be done' is a philosophy or concept that the aspirant tries to develop. One who can develop this philosophy and live by it, who can cultivate that spiritual strength and energy within, is recognized as a disciple, and eventually, in the course of time, as an enlightened being. The highest spiritual value to be cultivated in life is samarpan. The moment one lives that, yoga also reaches its point of culmination.

The final reward: perfect contentment
The aspirant on the path of surrender should try to remain unruffled, detached from all mental notions of good and bad. He must detach continuously by remembering that he is a heavenly soul. He should be wary of his mind, which is trying to drag him away. He should not care for recognition or strive to be seen as important. He should not worry about what others say or whether the world approves of him or not. The real devotee does not murmur, complain or grumble over the past. He is forever content.

Only when one has kicked off and thrown aside all wants and desires, doubts and brooding, every fear of being sullied, scared, insulted and praised, will one become the happiest person in the world. Let the body live in the world, but let the Atma, the spirit, rest in God. Surrendering the thoughts and desires to God is the key to supreme joy. Only after one realizes that one is an immortal child playing the eternal lila in the lap of eternity will one become really happy.

No one except a bhakta is really happy. *Avidya*, ignorance, causes darkness. Darkness causes fear. Fear causes confusion. Confusion causes objects. Objects cause craving. Craving causes indulgence. Indulgence causes samskaras. Samskaras cause birth and death and again rebirth. These three cause unhappiness and unrest in the depth of the soul. In order to be really happy, one has to cut the very roots of avidya by absolute surrender of the ego. One has to live a simple life.

A simple life is a blessing because it makes one free from cravings, desires and worldly attachments which cause pain and suffering. However, a simple life should not be equated with an ignorant and foolish life. One should go deeper and realize why a simple life is advised. As long as there are personal desires, even spiritual life will remain a matter of ambition and innumerable problems will be perceived. Thinking that one has problems means life is not understood in the light of divine will. When one is able to surrender, it can be seen that there are no real problems in life.

The secret of happiness is to understand, or at least appreciate, the mysteries of divine will, the laws of creation and karma. At the end of the Mahabharata war, when Lord Krishna was about to return to his kingdom in Dwaraka, his aunt, Kunti, mother of the Pandava brothers, the victors in the war, began pleading with him not to leave. Lord Krishna replied, "The war is over. My work is complete. Your sons have been victorious and the throne belongs to them. My duty is over, my obligations fulfilled."

Kunti beseeched him, "O Lord, now that we have material wealth and a vast kingdom, You are leaving us. It is better to live in suffering, poverty and destitution because then You are always present among us, always in our hearts and minds. Who is more important to us, God or matter? You are our Reality. O Krishna, if I had the choice, I would ask for the same distress to come again, so that You would remain with us."

There comes a moment in one's life when the world has no value, when one sees the futility of amassing material wealth as if it is an end to itself. If matter is an end, then life has no purpose. Kunti realized that suffering has a spiritual purpose, that it is the will of God, to help mankind realize a higher purpose in life. When one is in pain, one remembers God. God is present when there is suffering and distress. Whether in pain or pleasure, distress or comfort, God should never be forgotten.

This means that the whole philosophy of life has to be changed. From the very beginning, man has been taught to love pleasure and hate pain. In yogic philosophy, it is said that experiences born of the senses and sense objects end in pain. The wise do not accept them as reality, for they have a beginning and an end and are, therefore, not permanent. The experience, whether pleasant or painful, comes to an end.

To go beyond the limitations of these experiences, to go beyond dissatisfaction, one must try to perceive the universal aspect of the creation of which one is a part. When this perception comes, problems that appear not only in the lives of worldly people, but also in sincere spiritual aspirants will cease. Therefore, one may take to yoga or other spiritual practices, but there has to be a very important and central philosophy: "Thy will be done." When this philosophy emanates from the depths of one's being, then whatever one faces in life becomes a matter of joy, not a psychological or psycho-emotional problem. The aspirant is then able to bear all life's difficulties in the same spirit. That is the path of the gods, not the path of ordinary men.

16
Role of the Guru

Samarpan is an intangible experience which springs from the very depths of one's being at a certain point of spiritual evolution, when one wants to lose oneself in something larger. To catch hold of this fleeting experience many try to immerse themselves in nature, poetry or God, yet more often than not it eludes them. It is crucial to understand that to arrive at this state means the end of a journey and the beginning of a new road. There has been a glimpse, but the full experience is yet to come.

Here the guru plays an important role. He is the tangible manifestation of the aspirant's innate longing to surrender to a higher reality. The intensity of the aspirant's feeling brings him to his guru, for the fullness of surrender is rarely achieved without the guiding light of a superior being.

Most aspirants who come to a guru, therefore, carry a spark of samarpan in their hearts. However, as one's association with the guru grows and his expert hands chisel away at the personality, one realizes how frail the quality of one's surrender was, how rigid the mind, how insidious the ego, and how vital the guru. Surrender to God is at best an idea for the spiritual neophyte, but in the presence of the guru it becomes a living experience, although not necessarily an easy one.

Who is the guru?

The guru is the one who guides the disciple's life systematically, the one who steers the boat. In order to learn how to surrender to God, one must first have a guru. Surrender needs to be practised first with the guru, for without the grace of guru the path of surrender is not easily discovered. One needs to have that connection through which grace can flow. Without a living connection, without a guru, it is very difficult to connect with the subtle Supreme Reality, and receive His grace. The disciple's relationship with the guru is the test of the disciple's sincerity and devotion. In submission, however, the disciple is not throwing away his personality, but rather offering his limited self to one who will change it into the infinite Self. God takes over from there.

The guru and disciple are strangers to each other in the beginning, but the disciple finds faith in the guru. First, he practises surrender and belief in the guru and finally in God. He starts learning the A, B, C of surrender through the guru and develops it with continuous practice. In this faith, he sees the shadow, reflection and splendour of God. When, through practice, one's faith becomes strong, clear and divine, when it is generated through a pure mind and heart, one sees God. Then God, who was defined in various ways by other people, becomes apparent. The *Guru Stotram* says:

Gururbrahma gururvishnuh gururdevo maheshvarah.
Guru is Brahma, guru is Vishnu and guru is Shiva.

Guru is Brahma because he creates for his disciple a new and wondrous world; he is Vishnu because he sustains and protects him; he is Shiva because he annihilates the world of individuality. All great saints have underlined the necessity of a guru. It has also been said in the *Ramacharitamanas* that no one can cross the ocean of samsara without the guru's help, even if he is Brahma or Shiva.

The guru represents two realities: the teacher and the all-permeating Essence. The guru is both the teacher and the being who dwells in the disciple's heart. As a teacher he can teach, and as the indweller of the heart he guides the passages of the disciple's evolution and spiritual fulfilment. A true guru-disciple relationship is an experience of union with the inner spirit, which makes one go deeper into oneself and brings one closer to God. It is an experience that completely stupefies one.

From a practical point of view, the guru is qualified to tell the disciple how to practise surrender because he has undergone the entire process himself. There must have been a time when he was affected by mental agitation, faced conflicts and was pulled by the passions of life. Based on how he managed and overcame the situations, he can guide his disciples through their mental and emotional experiences. It is obviously safe to seek the help of a person who has undergone the same experience as oneself, and mastered it.

How does the guru bring about samarpan?
One cannot know the level of one's consciousness or the faults that lie within. One may try to correct one's social and mental faults, but there are faults embedded deep within the personality. Therefore, the guru often performs an operation on the disciple known as egodectomy, removal of the ego. This operation is so difficult that many disciples cannot bear it. However, if it succeeds, then they reach the goal. Surgery on the ego can be achieved by surrendering oneself to God also, but God is much too kind. Guru is a very hard person; he knows his duty; he knows how each and every individual should live, think and act. He does everything to pulverize the ego of the disciple. One may not understand this unless one becomes a disciple. The ego is the barrier between the individual and divinity, between disciple and guru. It is a very hard nut to crack; it is the 'I' which can sometimes be very subtle. It is because of the ego that complete surrender becomes difficult. The greater the ego, the lesser the receptivity. As the ego becomes subtler, the receptivity becomes greater.

By serving the guru ceaselessly, the ego of the disciple is effaced. He no longer thinks, "I came to my guru for self-realization and he is only getting me to clean the toilets! He has an unpaid servant in me." The guru creates conditions so that the disciple may purify himself. He also gives sadhana that will aid the process. In the course of time, the disciple's ego is gradually curbed and surrender occurs spontaneously. All one's worldly ways and abnormalities end; the external current is switched off and the internal light comes on.

There is an awakening which comes only when one has totally laid down one's arms. The surrender of disciple to guru is not like the surrender of a servant or a war prisoner, but once the disciple has surrendered, he knows it and says, "Take my life and do what you will." The true guru does not make his disciple surrender the world, but his limited self, the veil of ignorance that hangs between his ego and the all-pervasive reality.

The guru also continuously tests the disciple's sincerity and devotion, for he has to make sure that the disciple's mind will not shake at any moment. It is very important that the guru to be able to handle the disciple without any difficulty. If the disciple does not respond to the guru's instructions, suggestions or inspiration at the ordinary intellectual level, then how can the guru direct him in the higher realms? The guru should be able to influence and direct his disciple's mind, his conscious thinking, in any direction: right, left, down into the ditch, up on to the mountain, into fire or water.

For that purpose, the guru gives the disciple different exercises to check whether his awareness is responding and how far he has progressed on the path of surrender. Disciples realize the quality of their faith only when the guru presents them with certain difficult tests. This is especially true of sannyasin disciples who live with him, who have a total relationship with him. At a certain time during their stay, they are tested. At that time the disciple who passes is the one whose faith does not break. The guru gives him something in the form of a reward. It is called *guru kripa*, guru's grace.

A teacher, an acharya, can help one learn asana, pranayama and simple meditation practices, but such a master has limitations. Only the guru without limitations knows how to lead the ignorant and the blind to the path of self-realization by opening their third eye. A disciple may be academically intelligent, may have the highest of faculties and immense wealth, but his spiritual eyes are not yet open due to the veil of illusion or ignorance, *maya* or *avidya*. Only the guru can help one develop inner vision. Self-purification and karmic dissolution start in the service of guru. The disciple can carry on sadhana only in the conscious realms, while the guru helps him in the unconscious. He opens the closed door for the disciple and makes self-awakening possible. As the disciple develops his relationship with the guru, based on *bhakti* and *shraddha*, devotion and faith, an awakening begins to take place within him. The external guru helps to awaken the inner guru; he acts as a detonator to explode the guru tattwa within.

When the awakening begins, a transformation comes about in the structure of the mind and consciousness. It is not just a change, but a complete metamorphosis akin to a dog becoming a horse. The mind becomes entirely different; the structure of thinking undergoes a total transformation in quality, form, assessments and values. At the same time, perception or inner cognition becomes very subtle; one is able to apprehend the subtle essence. In this enlightened state of existence come revelations and inspirations, and a clear-cut path unfolds before one. One realizes what is to be done. If Nature has chosen one to become a Christ, to lead thousands of people, to heal hundreds, one will do it. This is when the disciple becomes a tool, a medium, an instrument of the cosmic process.

What the disciple must do
There are three types of disciples and a guru ordains them for different purposes. There are the lay disciples or householders; sannyasin disciples or the monastic order;

and the interior disciples. For each type, surrender takes place in a different dimension. If the lay disciple surrenders through devotion, it is sufficient. He does not have to surrender his business, family and children to the guru, but he must offer true devotion so that the guru can help give him find peace of mind and right understanding.

The monastic disciple has to surrender his desires and worldly ambitions so that when he leaves monastic life, his entire personality has been transformed. Then he can become a very good messenger of the guru's teachings. The third category of disciple, the intimate disciple, has to surrender everything. Such disciples are very rare, never very many, and the guru selects them for himself. First this disciple is tested, and only those who prove worthy are taken in. These disciples offer everything.

In every type of disciple the one indispensable qualification for surrender is to carry out immediately and spontaneously the commands of the guru. The attitude must be as if some unknown and unseen power compels him to do the work. It is not for the disciple to judge whether he is qualified or competent to undertake the task. He should not even think how it will be possible to complete the task. The disciple who tries to assess his competence before undertaking a task loses his chance to utilize his hidden powers. That is why the disciple should carry out the commands without forethought. It will prove to be a great boon, because then he may enter into the subtle regions of consciousness. If in this sphere he acquires that good quality, then in the next sphere the same also happens. If the disciple's ordinary consciousness is coloured by opposition to the guru's commands, then he will find it difficult to go beyond the plane of ordinary consciousness.

There are two necessary conditions for surrender. The first is faith that one will be able to surrender, and the second is the awareness, "My guru is within me." To achieve these may require breaking the existing patterns of the mind. This is the first step towards samarpan. One must be able to lose one's engrossment in the imaginary problems the mind has imposed upon itself, whether neurosis, psychosis, schizophrenia, frustrations or disappointments. Faith allows this to happen; it solves many problems of the mind so one can proceed to experience the inherent truth. To get there, however, one must first accept oneself. One has to come to the point where one can say, "I can do nothing; I cannot renounce; I cannot control the mind. My mind is full of terrible thoughts; I have bad habits!" Such acceptance is humility, and with it begins the process of emptying oneself.

A disciple of a guru or a devotee of God has to be as humble as a blade of grass, egoless and totally submissive, as if he does not exist, as if he were a flute. A hollow piece of bamboo can be made into a flute, but only when there are no knots can it produce a sweet melody. As long as the individual exists, the guru cannot be in him. In order to allow the guru to function through him, the disciple has to empty himself. The process of emptying oneself is the only practice or sadhana a disciple has to undertake. "Before you, I do not exist. I cannot think. You think through me. I leave the choice of my life in your hands" – this state of mind has to be practised. After all, how long can one hold one's head high if it is full of arrogance and ignorance, conflict and duality? To rend this duality may take lifetimes. Maybe one's guru is not great. He may be an ordinary man, but when the disciple empties himself, surrenders himself completely in total humility and obeisance, things happen. If one surrenders the ego to others in this world, one is liable to be exploited and destroyed. But when one surrenders the ego to a person who is compassionate and one's well-wisher, life changes. This person is one's guru, the one in whom complete trust may be placed.

The surrender of sannyasa
The most important preparation for taking sannyasa is a willingness to dedicate oneself totally. A sannyasin is one who has dedicated, who has surrendered, who has given up

everything that he has and is not going to use for his own self. The day he takes the vow of sannyasa he takes the vow of trusteeship. Sannyasa does not only mean renunciation, it means trusteeship. A sannyasin is simply a trustee of his body, mind, ability, knowledge and money. They are not his, and are to be offered to the guru to fulfil his mission. Then a sannyasin becomes an instrument of the guru.

As long as a sannyasin has the attitude that: "I am the doer," "I am doing" or "I must do," he is functioning on the plane of duality, on the plane of ego, *ahamkara*. He is functioning with a limited philosophy and limited conceptions. Many sannyasins fail in surrender because their primary education in sannyasa is incomplete.

The purpose of taking sannyasa should be to realize through experience one's own infiniteness and to throw away the idea and experience of limitations. All one's resources, mental powers and emotional capacities will have to be harnessed towards the fulfilment of this goal. The sannyasin must surrender everything he has in order to fulfil that resolve. He has no other purpose in life. Once the sannyasin has achieved this particular objective, then there is a realization of what he should do as his mission for the good of humanity. This mission cannot be a sannyasin's first idea, and aspirants should not lose track of this point.

Samarpan in the guru-disciple relationship

There are two important moments of surrender in human life. One is when one surrenders to the lower instincts, to one's temptations and mental whims. That is the common type of surrender that most people make. Some people are afraid to surrender their ego because they fear they will lose their individuality. They are obviously not aware that they surrender their ego in so many other ways in life. The other moment of surrender is to the guru, the inner essence. If one is a true disciple, one surrenders everything to guru: emotions, brain, intellectuality, good and bad deeds, ego, vanity, past, present and future, security, fears and passions. Nothing belongs to the disciple; he gives everything of himself to his guru.

The outcome of the first surrender is pain, agony and frustration. The result of the second type of surrender is *ananda*, bliss. The devotee begins to feel that he is no longer alone. There is someone who has the most awe-inspiring love for him, not on a temporary basis, but for eternity, and one begins to feel that the two are somehow one. This realization of unity is the consequence of the disciple's surrender to guru. This losing of oneself is not like death; it is passing over the threshold into higher experience.

Where do guru and disciple unite? Not on a physical, emotional or mental plane, but in total darkness, when everything is finished, in the innermost chamber where everything is dead. There one does not hear a sound or see any form or vision. One is aware of nothing but the guru, shining like a lofty light. That is how guru and disciple must commune with each other, and for that the disciple's ego must be annihilated.

When salt or sugar are mixed with water, the duality ceases; there is no longer any separate identity. That has to be the relationship between God and devotee, and between the guru and his disciple. This is only possible when there is perfect communion between them on the spiritual plane. Body, mind and emotions are temporary; the spirit is eternal and the relationship with the guru should be based on the spirit. If there is anything between the disciple and guru, it is between their spirits, not between their bodies or minds. It is not a physical, mental or emotional relationship. Initially, the relationship is established on emotional grounds because people belong to the emotional plane. However, the disciple has to step out of the emotional relationship, otherwise the sobriety, tranquillity, stability and homogeneity of the mind are lost.

A disciple's individual consciousness and the guru's individual consciousness have to merge into each other. This means that, except for the guru who is always with him, he is able to forget the whole world, whatever he is doing, thinking or feeling. That is communion on the spiritual plane. When one closes one's eyes, one sees the guru. When one cleans the bathroom, one feels him beside one. When one is planning some work, he is there in one's thoughts. One must have this *advaita bhava*, feeling of unity, with the guru.

The purpose of the guru-disciple relationship is to link with each other on a universal field, to be able to commune with each other. For this to happen the disciple must correlate his mental frequency with that of the guru. The individual mind is only a concept; it is nothing. There is no individual mind, only the universal mind. The universal mind is able to unite with every mind at any time and in any place. It is not a matter of transmission, but of communion and inter-union. Gurus have developed the universal mind, so they can operate anywhere. Every individual is a part of the universal mind, and when he is able to remove the ego, the barrier between him and guru, him and God, the individual and his inner essence, then the guru can communicate with him from any point and to any point because the two have the same mind. This has to be understood properly. It requires infinite patience on the part of the guru and infinite patience on the part of the disciple. Unless one has great faith and understanding and a sort of enlightenment within oneself, the communion cannot be established.

The relationship between guru and disciple is linked by faith. If there is no faith, there is no relationship. The guru is the reflection of the disciple's faith. If the faith of the disciple diminishes, he will see less of it reflecting from the guru. Therefore, to an ordinary disciple the guru plays the role of a kind mother, but shows his real nature only to disciples who have faith, for they are composed of a different material and can withstand the sharp chisel that cuts a beautiful form from a crude piece of wood.

It is to reaffirm the faith that exists in one's nature that emphasis has been placed on the guru-disciple relationship. This relationship is needed to fulfil the sublime aspect of life, and yet it is so difficult to maintain. Most disciples stay with the guru for a few years until they find some fault in him, and then they decide he is not their guru. This crisis occurs in a disciple's life when there is no faith. If the faith of the disciple is strong, the reflection from the guru will be very strong. The personality of the guru is the image of the faith of the disciple. Therefore, Mirabai has also said:

> *Now I have fallen in love with the guru's feet,*
> *I want nothing but the shelter of his sacred feet.*
> *The illusory world has now become a dream.*
> *For me the ocean of the world has dried up.*
> *Now there is no anxiety to cross it.*
> *The lord of Mira is the clever Krishna,*
> *And she is hopeful of the guru's refuge alone.*

If the disciple's faith is unshakeable and his belief is deep and strong, the guru's personality will dazzle him. Faith can be protected and developed by maintaining a consistent, intimate, indivisible relationship with the guru. For a very long time they live close to each other, until the disciple transcends the barriers of body and mind, until he transcends the nature of matter, and is able to communicate with the guru on an inner level. He develops intense awareness, total awareness, non-dual awareness of the guru on the spiritual plane. In the experience of samarpan in the guru-disciple relationship, the lower sphere of the mind is paralyzed so that the higher sphere becomes sensitive. When that happens, guru feels one with the disciple and sees no difference.

In spiritual life, transcendental knowledge is only given to a disciple whose mind has lost every point of worldly and lower sensitivity, which is unreceptive to lower reflexes, but open to higher ones. The disciple begins to hear his guru's instructions in the unconscious when in deep meditation. Thus, the guru takes him beyond the dead end of the void in which the disciple is stuck and shows him the eternal light. The guru permeates the disciple's consciousness through and through, even if he does not want to. For the guru loves the disciple too. When a guru loves his disciple, he is always aware of him, always thinking about him; he suffers from a disciple neurosis. When the disciple loves the guru so much that he can think of nothing else, he has a guru neurosis. This is the first and last requirement for the attainment of samarpan. It is the strongest form of shakti. This awareness is love and it is a very powerful link.

17
Descent of Grace

If one wants to enter the temple of God, in the beginning external steps such as practices and rituals are beneficial. However, the supreme temple, Shiva's real dwelling, is only found within. External shrines are built of bricks and mortar; they are merely models of what people have experienced and envisioned within themselves, only expressions of what is found within. It is very important to know the way to the inner shrine, and only by entering can one know God as the deity dwelling there. As long as there is awareness of the external symbols, one is within the boundaries of the mind. In order to experience reality, these boundaries have to be transcended, because God is beyond the limited, finite mind.

There are many techniques which lead to the point or brink at which one has to jump over the mind. However, how to make this final jump cannot be taught. Up to this point the yoga practices given by one's spiritual guide, or any spiritual practice for that matter, can help. But beyond this point no spiritual practice can serve as a guide, and no book has ever been written about it. All spiritual pursuits and religious practices take one only to the edge of this boundary of material consciousness, but to go beyond surpasses all human power of communication. The aspirant alone must find the way.

Only grace can help one to transcend the mind. Spiritual life, divine life or yogic life is difficult to navigate because it is the inner path. It is entirely and utterly dependent on God's grace. When the mind soars high in inner life, the path is uncharted; one does not know which way to go. Nothing external can help, for the unfoldment is within, not without. All the treasures and riches of the world are within. God's grace is required every step of the way. It cannot be denied that in order to achieve something effort has to be made. Many things can be done to prepare oneself, but ultimately one is completely dependent on God's grace. It is His decision how one's life moves. If the aspirant is true to it, then he can accept whatever is given. The more self-illumination there is, the more the grace will flow. The little 'i' must go, then the big 'I' will dwell in the devotee.

Gaining grace

The way to attain His grace is satsang, remembrance and prayer. *Satsang*, being where God and spiritual life are glorified, or where there is singing of bhajan and kirtan, helps to purify the self and the inner environment. Satsang must be compatible with one's inner environment. The name of the Lord is the greatest gift one can have. One should try to keep one's mind firmly anchored in the name. It is the highest sadhana, and beyond the comprehension of the mind.

To receive God's grace one must aspire for purity. The heart must be kept clean. To invite God to dwell in ones' heart and to make sure that He continues to remain there and give His blessings, it is essential to clean the heart. How will the devotee know that his heart is clean? Ramakrishna Paramahamsa used to say that where there is dirt, flies come, where there is wealth, thieves come, but if there is a beautiful garden with a lake, blooming lotuses and chirping birds, everyone will come. Similarly, the aspirant can tell the quality of his heart by what he attracts. If the heart is clean, it will invite grace. Yet, the paradox is that God's grace does not come; it is always there. Nothing is possible without grace. No matter how long one works to remove the rubbish, it will not be possible without higher assistance. To think that one can do it alone is speaking the language of the ego. One may make the effort, but ultimately everything has to be left to God, because when His grace showers, all the rubbish of life is instantly removed, just as darkness is removed by the first rays of the sun.

Grace falls on everybody at all times, but people do not realize it. God's grace flows not only towards a saint, but towards every being. To be worthy of God's grace, one must become aware of His grace. In order to receive God's grace, one must be prepared to live in constant communion with Him, even if it means sacrificing the very best in one's life. It may be at the cost of social prosperity, it may turn one into a beggar, but when grace fills one's life, none of that matters.

All those who come to Him with pure devotion receive His grace. The Lord of the universe and infinite plenitude has no pride. He does not see how scandalous was His devotee's past life. He looks not at the conduct, qualifications, status, prosperity or learning. All He sees is devotion. Both a deceitful merchant and a debased criminal, when immersed in devotion, make God their own. No matter what one's standing according to the codes of social conduct, in the eyes of God it is devotion alone that counts. From the moment a person begins to worship God, his connection with his past, caste, family and social conduct is broken. God looks upon him only as His devotee. Samskaras from past births vanish or subside with the Lord's grace. When a devotee completely surrenders to God, all his miseries, ego and past are completely transformed. Like a servant, God protects whoever worships Him, for He is a devotee of His bhakta. He becomes the slave of the slave and applies Himself silently to his service. The way of God is such. One who realizes this truth realizes God's grace.

Ways of grace

There are signs which indicate that God is accepting the devotee. This, of course, depends on the groundwork that has been done. The aspirant does not know if God will really accept him. Everybody says that they love Him, but how does one know whether He is accepting that love? This is the weakness of any love. No matter how intensely a lover loves his beloved, a doubt always remains in the back of his mind. Does she really accept my love? Does she love me? This is the great tragedy in the life of every lover. There is a beautiful song by Rabi Balen:

> *This is the way of the world,*
> *Whosoever loves me*
> *Binds me with a string of love.*
> *But your intense love is peculiar,*
> *Its ways are quite new.*
> *You never tie me in the bondage of love.*
> *You keep me ever free.*
> *Other lovers do not leave my company*
> *For fear that I might forget them,*
> *But You are one*
> *Who does not show His face,*
> *And days pass.*
> *Your love is unique,*
> *Whether I call You in prayer or not,*
> *Whether I remember You or not,*
> *Your love always awaits my love.*

Sometimes the devotee may think that it does not matter whether or not God accepts and loves him. He just has to do his duty, just play his part in His divine plan. On the other hand, if one attains God's love, he gets everything. What is the form of God's love? The definition of God's love varies. The form in which grace manifests varies from person to person, especially for those immersed in worldly sorrows, who do not have the power to bear this sorrow. If a couple do not get the child they badly want, they will keep breaking their head against God's image. People sway on their swings of happiness and misery. Each person has his own desires, which are most important to him. When grace manifests, a childless person is given a child and an incurable disease is cured. People accept these instances as God's grace.

It has been said in the *Srimad Bhagavatam*: "One who experiences Thy grace deeply, eagerly, every moment, who enjoys the pleasures and pains destined by karma, with a clear mind, and surrenders totally with a heart full of love, a body full of delight – he becomes qualified for liberation, just as a son becomes the heir to his father's property."

There are many examples which provide evidence of a higher power working in every sphere of one's life. Consider this. At night a person goes to sleep and in the morning wakes up, but in between there is a gap, a total void. When he wakes up, how does he know that he is the same person that existed yesterday? Although there is a total gap in which there is no continuity of identity, he never loses his identity. What is this process, and who carries it out? If one listens to a speech, one is able to immediately understand the speaker. What is the process of understanding? What is it that enables this simultaneous understanding? If this is not His grace, then what is? A person who thinks he is responsible for his own existence is the greatest fool!

Divinity exists within every being. Without His grace one could never live, breathe or think. A person eats food and the bones are strengthened, without any effort being made other than swallowing the food and discarding the waste product. Who is carrying out the processes of catabolism, anabolism, metabolism and assimilation? It is Him alone. This revelation in itself will humble one's ego.

Grace and effort

Only when total surrender becomes part of one's life does one begin to live in the spirit of God. Before that one is walking in the world and trying to be spiritual. Only by complete surrender can the grace of god be drawn down. The devotee must feel the grace at every step and surrender to it.

Nothing happens without God's grace. Whatever one receives, whatever one's successes in life, it is all His grace. Everything is an expression of that universal law. It is the supreme law. It is an omnipotent, omniscient and omnipresent law that controls every aspect of one's life. A true devotee receives guidance every step of the way. Everything is His grace. Initially one may think it is one's inner being who is speaking, the super soul giving guidance. Who is one's super soul? God is the first and the last. Everything is the grace of God, whom one has not seen and perhaps will not even see in the future. That realization must dawn.

Whatever is achieved in spiritual life is due, not to personal effort or diligence, but to God's grace. Not external things, but that which is eternal has only been given by the Lord. When there is grace, nothing is impossible. Tulsidas has said: "I prostrate at the lotus feet of Lord Hari by whose grace a lame person can cross mountains, a blind person can see, a deaf person can hear, a mute person can speak and a penniless person becomes king."

The *Bhagavad Gita, Srimad Bhagavatam*, other scriptures and all philosophies discuss this question: if God is the doer, then what is an individual's role? However, no one has been able to give a final answer as yet, so it can only be discussed. People look for a conclusive answer to this question, but they will not find it because their mind is not ready for it. When one does get the final answer, the questioner will have ceased to exist.

Whatever happens in an aspirant's life is not due to his own effort, his *purushartha*. Even without any effort, it will happen. Yet he makes the effort, because that in itself is a part of the will of God. This is an important point. If God wants one to achieve, it is impossible not to make the effort. God gives the inspiration to make the effort; he gives the mind with which the effort can be made.

Everyone has to do purushartha, to exert, whether or not fate exists. The train will arrive at the station at its prescribed time, not earlier. One has to fill in the time somehow. One receives whatever has been decided by destiny. The question arises therefore: why is effort necessary? The individual has to exert because he cannot exist without action. What will he do if he does nothing? If he gets money, a house and everything else that he wanted, what will he do? People work out of a sense of self, out of their ego, *ahamkara*; they work because life demands work, because work is an inseparable part of life.

Destiny and purushartha are two different things. One will receive from destiny whatever one has to receive. The work that one does, the effort one makes in life, is the need of the ego. It is all His grace. We are dependent on grace. The aspirant may try everything possible in spiritual life. Eventually, when the desires are exhausted, he says, "God, I am tired. I can do nothing more." Then he renounces everything that can be considered his accomplishments. He surrenders to God like a defeated soldier. He receives amnesty from God.

If one can remain without action, there is no problem. One works for as long as one needs to work. When one can live without desires, thoughts, worries, without feeling any sense of responsibility, when a person attains this state, he can give up work and depend exclusively on God's grace.

18

Living Samarpan

The life of a bhakta who has achieved samarpan, who is living the divine connection, is guided by practical actions of responsibility, nobility, grace and dignity. He is not merely immersed in singing and repeating God's name, but the depth of his devotion manifests in his qualities, behaviour and actions in relation to other beings. In the twelfth chapter of the *Bhagavad Gita*, Lord Krishna describes the essence and the spiritual nature of a bhakta. Similar descriptions can also be found in the *Narada Bhakti Sutras*, *Nirvanopanishad* and *Srimad Bhagavatam*. To live samarpan is to live the qualities enumerated in these scriptures, and just as samarpan is a sadhana, perfecting these qualities is also a sadhana. Rare is the aspirant who reaches the state of unequivocal surrender and rare is the soul in whom the transcendental qualities of a bhakta have fully blossomed. To know who a bhakta is, therefore, is to know one's goal. It is an indication of how far one has made it into the journey and the distance that remains to be charted.

A *bhakta*, a devotee, who lives in samarpan has transcended the detrimental forces of the personality and is no longer troubled by envy, jealousy or resentment. He is a friend to all; he has no enemies. He does not identify with the body or with worldly matters, and therefore he is free from false conceptions of ego and doership. He is never disturbed by circumstances. He is always calm, quiet and patient, despite encountering distressful situations. He is a perfect mystic, attuned to the universal or cosmic consciousness. His senses are controlled and he is absorbed in devotional service. Nothing can turn his head or heart away from the object of his love. *Adhimitra*, intense earnestness, manifests in him, an extremely strong urge to unite with the Beloved. Such earnestness makes a devotee so intent on achieving his goal that he cannot let go of it or rest until he achieves it.

It is not enough for a devotee to merely practise classical emotional bhakti or only the social virtues. He needs to combine both aspects of devotion, for it is only when the two forms are blended together that the state of union becomes perfect. In order to achieve this, the scriptures describe several attributes which the bhakta must perfect.

Self-restraint
A true bhakta is able to control his temperamental reactions and impulses. To rejoice, to hate, to grieve, to desire and to be influenced by the effects of karma are natural and temperamental actions of human beings. Therefore, it is said that a devotee must have the self-control to overcome these natural impulses. It is through the process of discipline, by controlling the unruly manifestations of the personality, that one can stay on the spiritual path.

If the aspirant has mental restraint, then that serves as his protection, security and comfort. Some aspects of mental restraint are complete control over and total clarity of the mental faculties, which leads to knowledge of justice and injustice, discrimination and awareness. In such restraint there is harmony, continuity and discipline in the structure of the mind, emotions, psyche and spirit.

Self-restraint is the keyword here. Without continued effort, the state of self-restraint, restraint of the inner senses, will not be attained. There are six inner sensory organs, consisting of the *karmendriyas*, five organs of action, and *manas*, the rational mind. The five karmendriyas are the inner attributes of *buddhi*, the discriminating aspect of the mind, and pertain to the dimension of logic and understanding, the process of interaction between an individual and the external world. Manas is the aspect which observes the interaction of the five sensory organs and assimilates them, thinks about them and refers to their experiences as its knowledge. Restraint of these inner senses is the code of conduct followed by a yogi and bhakta.

Discrimination

The aspirant has to constantly move in the direction of discrimination, *viveka*. Discrimination is having the ability to discern the real from the unreal. Viveka is neither a mental nor a physical experience; it is beyond both the physical and the mental, beyond mind and speech. Discrimination is an awareness that can only come through living with a discerning spiritual consciousness, and learning to manage the experiences that life presents.

What sustains the state of samarpan is the disciple's viveka. His discrimination is his protection against being caught in the web of samsara, from the evanescent world and changing appearances. He uses reflection to help him walk along the path. If one has discrimination, one will always strive to know the real, and not be caught up in the unreal. This ability to discriminate between real and unreal prevents one from losing awareness. The world can offer anything, and from that one will be able to select what is beneficial, real, true and just, and leave aside all that is unnecessary, impermanent and unreal.

Equanimity

The highest devotee is one who has attained equanimity, who is mentally balanced in the company of both friends and enemies, in honour and dishonour, in heat and cold, in pleasure and pain, and free from association with worldly objects. Praise and reproach are alike to him. He knows that nothing is stationary in life. Disturbances as well as dissatisfaction are mental reactions, which flow like a stream into a river. They are lost in the past. This devotee is silent, contented with whatever he has, without attachment to home, and steady of mind.

Real life is beyond the limits of the mind. The mind is the seat of various pleasant and unpleasant feelings. The mind is the womb of *sukha*, happiness, and *dukha*, suffering. Mental balance is a sadhana, a means to an end. Equilibrium is different from endurance. It is a quality of understanding the futility and perishability of every event. Equilibrium is that quality where one's Self has become the witness of all events. As long as one considers oneself to be a doer, one must enjoy as well as suffer the consequences. Therefore, the bhakta views everything with equal vision. He is not subject to ups and downs, fluctuations and dissipations, or the changing biological rhythms that govern an ordinary person's conduct. There is perfect coordination between his senses, thoughts, feelings and discrimination. His life expresses the divine calmness that results from harmony in all spheres of life, from gross to spiritual. He has complete acceptance without the influence of desire or ego, and in this way is able to remain peaceful, despite the continuous interaction between consciousness and energy.

Consciousness and energy interact on many levels: physical, mental, emotional, psychic and spiritual. However, because the aspirant's individual identity has been completely surrendered or dissolved with the attainment of discrimination and detachment, the illusory, unreal or sensory world of consciousness and energy, and their interaction, play, or *lila,* dissolves, and one experiences the self-luminosity of enlightened awareness. This results in purity, balance and equilibrium in thought, word and action. In that pure state of being the soul resides in its own nature, which is bliss and oneness with the spirit. There is no support from the external sensory attractions, by the perceivable world, universe or cosmos.

An angry man once began abusing Lord Buddha. Buddha listened very carefully to the abuse, and when the man had finished, asked him only one question: "What would you do if you gave someone a gift and he refused to accept it?" The abuser replied, "I would take the gift back." Buddha said, "In the same manner, I do not accept your abuse. Please take it back." Buddha had perfected equanimity.

Freedom

One's nature in the state of samarpan is that of a *tyagi*, one without ties or attachment to his own karma which brought him into this birth. There are fourteen aspects of the human personality which usually always travel with one from birth to death: the five *karmendriyas* or organs of action, the five *jnanendriyas* or sensory organs and the four mental aspects: *manas*, the analytical mind, *buddhi*, the discriminating mind, *chitta*, the subconscious mind, and *ahamkara*, the egocentric mind. For the tyagi, these ties to his human birth have no power. They do not tie him down in any way. He is beyond their influence. He is liberated from them. He has been released from the prison of his limited mind, and is free from all the changing mental conditions and tribulations. He has become a *mukta*, liberated.

Mukti means a state of no bondage, a state of freedom and contentment. This state comes about because the aspirant is free from all craving for enjoyment. Even desires in the form of seeds are completely absent from his nature. This contentment in a *para bhakta*, a supreme devotee, is not what is understood by satisfaction or gratification of desires. This state does not necessarily dawn after cravings have been fulfilled; rather, it is an outcome of the realization that objects can never gratify the senses. Therefore, he renounces the attachments of the world, the cravings of the body, the craving for pleasure and repulsion from pain. Having renounced all these and having become detached from the world of objects and senses, the aspirant has no base anywhere. He is free from every kind of earthly, material, sensory and mental bondage.

From the spiritual point of view, having a desire can be the basis for attraction, attachment or bondage. One who has surrendered everything is free from all cravings and desires, and is not bound to one place in the spectrum of the mind, nature or consciousness. Such an aspirant is free to turn his existence to the will of the Divine.

A friend to all
In addition to dedicating his life to realization of God, a bhakta is also recognized by another great virtue. Not only is he free from mental agitation, but other people are also not agitated by his personality. This serves a double purpose: social peace and personal peace. He does not become impatient because he dwells in the Absolute; he lives in a dimension which is not limited by time. Every action he performs becomes a creative activity, an activity of joy, pleasurable to himself and to others. His activities are selfless and contribute to the spiritual upliftment of humanity. He has gone beyond self-centred ideas, fears and insecurities and lives in the present, expressing himself in an integrated manner, without harming anyone or anything. His conduct has divine calmness and self-restraint, and his compassion reaches out to all.

The word *bhakti* is derived from the root word *bhaj*, which means to serve, and in a broader sense to serve both God and humanity. Traditionally, bhakti means prayer, worship, meditation and adoration of God's transcendental form. In a broader sense, however, the word means service of both God and humanity. From this point of view, any endeavour that a devotee undertakes is only to fulfil or enhance his devotional service. There is no other purpose for his existence. He expects nothing from anyone, but is an impartial friend to everyone.

When one is established in samarpan, then one may live like a normal person, but one's intentions and motivations, the direction of the flow of one's energies have changed. Previously they were selfish, now they have become selfless, previously they were self-oriented and self-centred, now they have become universal and expansive. Previously one would only think of one's own pleasure and happiness, now one begins to think of the pleasure and happiness of others. One acquires *atmabhava*, the ability to see oneself reflected in others. One begins to serve others.

Live in the world, but be not of it

The pure devotee is able to live in this world, but be not of it. He is like the lotus, which grows out of water, but is water-resistant. In the same way, the actions and life of a devotee take place in the mortal world, but his enlightened awareness does not belong to the mortal dimension. His only possessions are brahmacharya and peace. His first possession is that he is established in Truth, and his second possession is peace. The lives of King Janaka and Lord Rama illustrate this state of being. Like these inspiring figures, a devotee should be able to manage his mental conditions while maintaining his devotional attitude as he goes about life. He needs to integrate individual mental peace with individual devotion. If he ignores his own mental conditions, as many do, he is sure to face an emotional crisis, which will ultimately result in a spiritual crisis.

The state of mind of the realized bhakta is the state of *unmani*, the threshold between complete internalization and complete externalization, having the vision of both. His awareness is developed to the extent that the internal and external worlds are experienced simultaneously. With the body he lives in the external world of the senses, while with the soul he lives in the inner world of spirit. This state of being on the threshold is attained through self-effort made for realization, through yoga.

Understand the nature of maya

If a devotee is affected every now and then by the fluctuating impulses of his nature, then maya will drag him down to lower planes of the body, mind and senses, where he may become bound to the effects of *prakriti*, manifest nature, and the three *gunas* or attributes.

Everything related with the world and the mind is conditioned by the interplay of the three gunas, of sattwa, rajas and tamas, but realization is not conditioned by them.

It is an experience free from all conditionings and influences. The world that is seen as manifest in ordinary consciousness is actually impermanent when viewed from a higher perspective. The human body complex is a framed network of delusion, infatuation and gunas, which go on changing. Only the Absolute Reality is permanent because it is unchanging and free from the gunas and delusion.

In the domain of prakriti, the opposites predominate. However, union gives knowledge of the opposites. One who has experienced union is active, not reactive, for union gives knowledge and understanding of positive and negative, justice and injustice, good and evil, past and future. When the mind is stabilized, oneness is experienced. Nature is not split into two; the opposites are different manifestations of the same prakriti.

One tends to identify with what is portrayed and experience the corresponding emotions of sorrow, joy, like, dislike, etc. This is false identification, which is akin to watching a movie or a stage play. One forgets that one is a mere spectator of what is taking place. In the same way, the soul or self is only a witnessing consciousness, but it has forgotten its true nature, and is identifying with the mind and its patterns or modifications so deeply that it cannot extricate itself. Maharishi Patanjali recommends different techniques in the *Yoga Sutras* to cater for the differing temperaments of individuals so that the mind stuff can be brought into a state of equilibrium and peace. In that state, the self becomes aware of its true, universal and divine nature.

The essential teaching that a worthy disciple receives is that this world hides a different reality, the reality of spirit, the reality of divinity. There may be a thousand ways of identifying the Divine for a normal person involved in the world, but these ways are manifestations of only one reality, and that is what one has to realize. In order to understand that divine reality, the disciple has to learn that what is perceived as real in this gross dimension of consciousness is not the Absolute Reality; it is only an appearance, and hides the essential reality. One must separate oneself from the normal experiences, habits, attachments, situations and conditions of life. One must achieve disunion from worldly life through non-attachment, *vairagya*.

The disciple who realizes the changing or transitory nature of the entire creation is one who has absorbed the teachings and identified the Supreme Being as the non-changing, eternal reality. He has renounced fear, attachment, grief and anger, which relate to the gross mind, the subtle mind and the emotions, and therefore act on the personality in different ways, transforming and changing one's lifestyle and habits. One who has universal vision has no need of them. He has burned all illusion, possessiveness and ego and, therefore, has uprooted his karma.

In order to do this and free himself from the clutches of prakriti or maya, he has made effort through sadhana to dissolve or surrender his ego expressions in the form of possessiveness, attachment, craving, desire, ambition, anger, hatred, jealousy and greed, etc. Once these experiences of ego have been subdued, then the illusory world dissolves. As long as he was influenced by the senses and the mind, his karmas could not be uprooted. One may be able to perceive the inner self during meditation practices, but unless the influences of the mind and senses cease to have an effect, karmas will never be uprooted. This can only happen through self-effort in the sadhana of daily life, using discrimination and detachment. In this process, the limited self is dissolved and surrendered, but the Atma, the permanent, real Self, is not affected by the change to the gross self. The identity of the Self as an all-encompassing reality remains unaffected.

Surrender

When the senses and mind are under control, harmony and integration are attained. That is the state of *sanyam*, action with discrimination and non-attachment. The faculty of viveka, discrimination or right understanding, develops along with vairagya, non-attachment, towards the sensory world. There is no shutting off from worldly experiences, but complete acceptance, which has no positive or negative influence on the mind or personality. Normally, if one receives good news, one feels happy and if one hears sad news, one experiences grief. That happens because of self-identification. When the individual identity is surrendered, the illusory world of prakriti also dissolves.

Ultimately, the path is shoonya. *Shoonya* means nothingness, the dropping away of everything, both material and physical. It is the state where there are no signposts along the way. Through discipline one can train oneself to experience such a state. Once one reaches shoonya and has dropped everything, all that remains is the authority of the Supreme. Self-effort ceases completely and one moves according to the music being played by the Divine.

The devotee knows that he is simply an instrument and that life is being played through him by the supreme musician. He accepts whatever happens as an experience of life and exists on whatever is given without any manipulation to attain it. He is neither the doer nor the enjoyer. He is being guided. Individual identity dissolves and gives way to the experience of oneness. There is homogeneity or harmony in all expressions; no individualistic traits remain. Self-identification with the body and mind no longer exists. Only one continuous flow of consciousness is experienced. For one who has experienced such oneness, the eternal fear of losing one's identity, of not wanting to be controlled by someone else's thoughts, no longer exists. Having attained universality, he knows and experiences the non-doership of the self, and knows that he is being guided by a higher force. He flows with the will that is guiding him, and this ability to flow with the divine will is real surrender. People say, "I surrender myself, my body, heart and spirit," thinking that from the next day onwards they will follow the guru's every instruction, but this is duping oneself.

It is a rare bhakta who is able to achieve true surrender. It requires purity of mind, complete sense control and desirelessness. All these are necessary before one is competent enough to reach the goal of absolute surrender. Realization comes from within. It cannot be comprehended by an ordinary mind coloured by likes and dislikes, and it is to such people that instructions for enlightenment are given. St Francis was able to do it, and he prayed to the Lord, "Make me an instrument of Thy peace." When Krishna was asked why the flute was so dear to him, he said, "It is hollow inside, so I can play it as I like." The true bhakta has become hollow. All works are performed as worship of God. He has surrendered his body, mind, soul and actions as flowers at the feet of the Lord. He is ever absorbed in the Lord, he has lost himself in God-consciousness through total self-surrender. That is his last and advanced stage.

Rest in the supreme consciousness

A true devotee is able to feel God's presence in all beings and manifest it in every interaction in his life. He is able to uphold this vision of God alongside his personal love for God. It is not difficult for him to feel that the whole world is a manifestation of God. However, if this is only a philosophical feeling, it will not serve the devotee to the last point of realization, and union with the Divine will not be experienced.

A true disciple demonstrates the Supreme Reality in his very conduct because he has realized and established it in his life. This realization is not something that he has understood intellectually or read about in a book. He has experienced the Supreme Reality and his entire being has been transformed by that experience. He lives in communion with the Self, with divine consciousness, and therefore whatever he does is a demonstration of the higher reality. He has inner vision of the Divine, of Brahman, God, and this is recognized by aspirants seeking to attain the same. Prosperity permeates his entire being, not physical or material prosperity, but cosmic and spiritual abundance. He is united with the divine consciousness and rests totally in that state without fear, in complete relaxation.

He realizes that whatever is going on in the world is but the divine sport of the Lord, His *lila*. He realizes the truth of the utterances in the *Brahma Sutras*: *Lokavattu lila kaivalyam*.

He feels he is one with the Lord and is a partner in His lila. He lives for Him only. He lives in Him only. His thoughts and actions are now of God Himself. The veil has dropped. The sense of separateness has dissolved.

In that state of universality, after one has attained realization of the divine consciousness, when one is experiencing the dimension of the divine or spiritual consciousness, when ego identity of body and mind or individuality has been destroyed, there is no place for any ego expression. This state is a pure field, where no earthly weed can grow. When there is 'I' consciousness, desires and actions become the seeds which will grow in the form of weeds, grass, shrubs and trees. However, if the ego, which is the basic ingredient for the growth of these weeds, is destroyed, then there is no ego related with individuality.

One with God
Once the vision of eternal reality is attained, the individual consciousness receives the gift of bliss, ananda. After this vision, everything is seen as God. Even this illusory world, which is the cause of pain and suffering, is seen as the garden of bliss. A person who has had that degree of realization will also have the knowledge and awareness that he has only one identity, which is the single identity of spirit, the feeling and experience of oneness with the spirit. He resides in bliss, in the solitude of oneness. He lives in the space of consciousness where there are no barriers, either individual or cosmic. There is just one eternal continuity, the state of being; not a state of becoming. That continuity, eternity or infinity is the truth which he has realized. He perceives the unifying aspect of everlasting bliss. Despite having the knowledge of positive and negative qualities, at this level of behaviour he expresses neither negative nor positive reaction. Knowing no boundaries, having no demarcations or defining limitations, he experiences the omniscient field of consciousness, universal consciousness, and has just the one experience of bliss, from which all thoughts and actions generate.

A bhakta who rests in God-consciousness has transcended the three ordinary states of consciousness: *jagrat*, the consciousness active in the manifest world; *swapna*, the consciousness active in the subtle world, during dreaming; and, *sushupti*, the consciousness active in the absence of awareness, in the state of deep sleep. He has attained the fourth state of *turiya*, transcendental consciousness, the experience of oneness of the Self. The previous states of consciousness have dissolved or merged, which results in the emergence of a new self, the one who is twice born.

The bhakta now lives in the state of turiya where there is communion with the supreme intelligence. He has discovered his formless form; he has transcended the three gunas, and destroyed illusion. All his cravings and other mental modifications have been burned. He is firm, steadfast, merged in the Supreme Being, established in Truth. Prakriti is just the covering which the soul or Atma, as enlightened awareness, has around itself. In this state of enlightened awareness he has become one with the eternal vibration, cosmic or universal consciousness. At that time, in the state of omniscience, omnipresence and omnipotence, the *anahata nada*, the unstruck sound, is the mantra.

The entity that such a bhakta worships is indefinable, and his state is indescribable. The devotee cannot give any description of his ultimate God, the divine being he worships, and of the state which he has attained. It is not possible because this state is beyond the description of the senses, beyond speech and sound, beyond any description of the mind. There is total dissolution of the physical and mental states of the devotee. He is one with the Divine and, therefore, his knowledge is complete. There is nothing for him to realize, to understand or to know. There is nothing that he can learn because he *is* knowledge. He is All. He is self-contained. If anything at all remains for him to do, it is to transmit the knowledge of the Self or Brahman. Now he is himself a source, a centre of learning, which does not have a structure, base, or the need of any institution or ashram.

19

Divine Communion

All desires are but forms of a single desire: to love and to be loved. In other words, there is a tendency in everyone to seek oneness and establish union, to experience love. There are two kinds of love. One is real or divine love, which is transmitted from the spirit, and the other is material love, in which there is an interplay of the mind and senses. Earthly, material love, which is empirical in nature, blinds one's vision; it is the cause of all pain and agony. Divine love, on the other hand, liberates one from all pain. Divine love manifests when surrender blossoms. It is a love that does not demand. It is dedication; it knows nothing but sacrifice. At the altar of divine love, one surrenders body and soul, indeed all that one had claimed to possess. 'I surrender' is the underlying theme of divine love; 'give me' is the watchword of an exploiter.

It has been said that a person who wants something in exchange for love is a seller of love. Such love is mere self-interest, not true love. But when divine love manifests, the devotee gives such self-interest a wide berth. The purpose of communion with God is no longer for the meaningless fulfilment of one's wishes or for superficial bhakti. It has no reason. It is love for love's sake, bhakti for bhakti's sake. It is *nishkama*, without any expectation of a reward or boon. Devotees who have this quality pray to God because they are in love with Him. They have nothing to ask of God, no selfish motive; they seek no benefits from God. They do not want happiness and success, solutions to their worldly problems or release from sorrow and suffering. They turn to God out of love for Him. Chaitanya Mahaprabhu, Mira, Hanuman and the gopis are examples of devotees who expressed such pure love.

Unity of awareness

Devotion and divine love are the same. When one loves an object of the world passionately, one's total being is directed towards the attainment of that aim, whether it is money, power or any other object. When one's mind is directed to God with devotion, the totality of one's consciousness is completely saturated, totally overpowered by the consciousness of God. Then a moment comes when the duality of consciousness is lost and one experiences a state of non-dual consciousness, an experience of unity with the beloved object of devotion. This unity of awareness is achieved in samarpan, when everything has been offered to God, when nothing blocks one's awareness of the innermost essence.

When devotion to God intensifies, a sense of bliss is experienced as one moves more and more into the wholeness of one's being, and nothing is seen as an 'enemy'. Negative thoughts are not harboured, but neither does one submit, flatter or sell one's soul. One is simply in the spiritual experience of the inner being. Everything is experienced as compassion and love, as a feeling of being in synchronicity. One is no longer the physical body; instead one becomes the consciousness that is expanding to include the whole of existence.

St Francis of Assisi was constantly in tune with everything. He could commune with birds and animals, for he saw God in everything. When the mind loves God, thinks of Him and lives in Him, then God is everywhere and in everything. It has been said, "Love all," for God is all and all is God. This can be understood if one can become one with nature, with the sun and the moon, the oceans and rivers, the valleys and forests, the birds and animals, the rocks and deserts. If one can appreciate and deeply immerse the mind in nature, if a bird in flight can take away one's mind, if a flowing river or flowers can make one forget one's tragedies, if the rising full moon can blow away one's emotions, if one feels like counting the stars, then everything one does is for the love of Him alone. That is the law.

During japa and meditation, kirtan and prayer, one may be able to practise such love. When one is all alone, really alone, one is with Him. In the stillness of one's own presence, one's own formless and eternal reality can be felt as an unmanifested presence which gives life to one's physical form. One can then experience the same feeling deep within every other human being and every other creature. This feeling is true love.

An all-consuming force

To be in love with the Divine means to be in a state where the soul rests in the blissful lap of the Divine. It is a state of being; it is not a feeling coming from outside, not dependent on a person or an external form. It is a state where all shades of emotion assume a concentrated form. Emotion is one force, but it has many channels. Some flow towards other people, objects, ambitions and affairs. When emotions are sublimated, they unite to form one force, just as many small streams converge to form a large river. In bhakti all channels of emotion are fused into one; it is an all-consuming force. It is one's inner attitude towards God and guru.

When bhakti awakens, the universe appears to be infinite and vast, and the devotee finds he is all alone. He knows not where he came from, nor where he is going. This is a psychic experience in one's life. However, devotion to God does not arise due to insecurity or loneliness; it comes when one realizes the limitations of all other forms of attachment. All other attachments are subject to conditions related to time, space and object; they have a beginning and an end. Only attachment to the Divine has no limits. It is a force which alleviates every worry and frees one from the thraldom of dissatisfaction and spiritual unrest.

When the intensity of bhakti attains its peak, it becomes *para bhakti,* transcendental devotion, supreme devotion. If one has ever loved or hated intensely, one will understand what is meant by intensity of devotion in a para bhakta. It is like a boy with a beautiful, new girlfriend. No matter what he does, she is always before him. He may not see her, say her name or even think of her on a conscious level, but he is aware of her all the time on the subconscious plane of the mind. It is this quality of awareness of God that one must have. Bhakti is a feeling which is extremely strong, so strong that one is constantly aware of it. It is not a lukewarm attraction; it is so overpowering that nothing else exists in the mind. It cannot be forgotten, no matter how hard one tries. The feeling of love for Him overpowers the mind, whether one is asleep, awake, or even dreaming.

How does a small child feel towards his mother in her absence as well as her presence? A similar love and devotion must be awakened. Overwhelming, overpowering and intoxicating love is the secret. Like Chaitanya, Mira and Radha, one must awaken one's devoted and loving soul. Bhakti is an inexplicable attitude of devotion towards one's chosen form of God, *ishta devata.* It is not passion, lust or romance. It is an unceasing thirst for union with God.

Without intense devotion for Him, if one forgets Him for worldly interests, one will be unable to commune with Him. Surrender is a mockery if the aspirant lacks bhakti, love for God. As long as one is unable to surrender entirely and rest in His grace, as long as one is not overwhelmingly devoted to Him, no amount of fasting, pilgrimage, study of the scriptures and ritualistic worship and chanting will confer the divine experience. Everything can be obtained from the material world except love for Him. That love can only be awakened from within oneself. It is already there, trying to find an expression.

Love intensifies the process of spiritual growth, deepens the awareness and protects the aspirant from laziness as well as mental dissipation. The deeper the love, the more intense the awareness. Intense awareness helps to free the devotee from mentally drifting during sadhana. If there are fluctuations during sadhana, it means that the awareness is not intense and the love is not constant. However, if one fails to develop intense longing to unite with Him, it is the individual, not the mind, that it to blame. The individual has been unable to channel his dissipated emotions towards Him because his *bhava*, inner feelings, are insipid. Bhakti only asks the devotee to get rid of mental imbalance and spiritual ignorance.

Beyond the mind

Intellect is necessary to earn money, to manage a family or business, for education, industry and politics, but it has no place where devotion is concerned. The bliss that is experienced when one can surrender the limited self to the wholeness of life cannot be understood by the intellect or sensory organs. It is not ordinary happiness, excitement or joy. It is an all-encompassing sense of feeling good at a very intense level.

Philosophers and thinkers write about God in a manner which most people can never understand. They argue about Him, but do not realize how simple God really is. He is without complications and the need for intellectual attainment. It is not through the intellect, reading the scriptures or countless prayers that one will surrender everything to God. Even the most illiterate person with least awareness of the modern world can have inner vision or *darshan* of God and receive the miraculous from Him if he develops love for Him.

Without love, God cannot be seen. It is a kind of puzzle. One cannot say, "Let me see Him once, then I will believe." First, one must develop love for Him. Only then can He be seen, for the moment one loves, the eyes become blind. It is a different eye that sees: the third eye or inner vision. When love brims over, when it becomes spontaneous and overwhelming, then the eyes that see material objects no longer function. A different vision opens up, known as God vision. With the opening of inner vision, one can see God.

Once this path opens up, one's whole life becomes clear. It is like a green signal. One may continue to go to work in the morning, earn money, drive a car, eat food and participate in all the other activities of a normal working person. However, life is seen differently. Problems no longer perturb one, for there is the knowledge that God will help one through all life's situations. One no longer needs to say prayers, at least not those worded by the poets. Prayer is internal; it does not lie in words, but in feeling.

Many believers

The whole world can be divided into two groups. One believes in grace, contact or communion with God. It thinks, "The heat is due to God; my child is born due to God's grace; I have secured a good job due to God's grace." This group lives entirely by faith. The other group thinks, "Rain is the work of nature, but I can also create it; having a child is a natural process, but I can do something about it." Essentially, those who belong to this group depend on themselves and dominate much of the world. They do not believe that God does anything. He may be there, it may be one's duty to remember Him and bow down to Him sometimes, but as far as building the world, educating children or making decisions is concerned, they believe that they have to do it on their own.

One is either a gnostic or an agnostic; it is a matter of individual preference. People may go to a temple to pray when things are not going well. Three-quarters of the world is like that. However, as far as worldly problems are concerned, God should be kept out of the picture. He should only be a symbol of bhakti, not the support for one's insecurities, inabilities, inefficiencies or lack of confidence.

Gradually, believers in God should become prema bhaktas. In the *Bhagavad Gita* (7:16), it is said that there are four types of devotees, *bhaktas*, who worship God: arta, artarthi, jignasu and prema *Arta* refers to those who pray to God for relief from distress. *Jignasu* bhaktas are those who seek knowledge, who want to find answers to questions such as: 'What is transmigration', 'What is the meaning of the scriptures', 'What is God', etc. The third type is the *artharthi*, who wants a good job or good grades for his children, and therefore performs some anushthana or sadhana in a temple. The fourth type is the *prema* bhakta, whose devotion to God is only for the purpose of surrender and to become one with Him. Therefore, four types of devotees place their trust in God.

Arta, jignasu and artarthi bhaktas are very generous in their devotion to God; they pray, they give their heart to Him, they believe in Him. However, for the prema bhakta God is his very soul; he loves Him for the sake of love. To attain samarpan, it is better to be a prema bhakta.

Apara and para bhakti

The philosophy of bhakti divides the emotional expressions into two levels. The lower grade of bhakti is *apara bhakti*; the higher state of emotion is *para bhakti*, supreme or transcendental bhakti. Para bhakti and prema bhakti are one. When prema is the basis of bhakti, it turns into para bhakti. The saints have spoken on this point from the beginning of creation. The Sufis called it *ishk hakiki*, Christ called it divine love, Buddha called it *karuna*, Mahavira called it *ahimsa*. Chaitanya Mahaprabhu, Ramakrishna Paramahamsa, Kabir, Nanak, Surdas and Tulsidas have all spoken about it.

Apara bhakti involves ritualistic worship, undertaking pilgrimages, visiting saints, reading the scriptures, etc. It is said that everyone should perform the methods of apara bhakti, so that they receive inspiration and the mind becomes purified and one-pointed. Only then will they be able to discern the fact that all manifestations in life are a creation of the Divine, and that the individual 'I' is only an actor. This revelation comes after practising apara bhakti for many years, provided it is done correctly. Ultimately, when this realization dawns, para bhakti begins. The para bhakta considers his life not as his own, but as a manifestation of the divine will. The karmas he performs, the sufferings he undergoes, the pleasures he enjoys are all the divine will. That becomes the realization.

If practised unselfishly, apara bhakti will culminate in para bhakti. But if practised selfishly, for example, praying in a temple or church with a specific motive, it will not grow. Gradually, the understanding must dawn that it is not appropriate to pray to God for a wife, husband, children, money, health, etc. When this realization finally comes, the devotee begins practising unselfish bhakti, with the belief that everything belongs to Him. By this method one does not accumulate the results or influences of the karma one performs while living in the world. One becomes free from *prarabdha karma*. This happens only in the case of the highest bhaktas, not those who worship in temples or surrender merely through the intellect.

Para bhakti is not ordinary love; it is a state of union with the Divine. It is the divine love realized by Ramana Maharshi, Ramakrishna Paramahamsa, Paramahamsa Yogananda and many others. They experienced constant union with universal love. Para bhakti is the state of consciousness where the aspirant is united with God. It is the culmination of the sadhanas of bhakti yoga, jnana yoga, karma yoga, raja yoga and all the other yogas. All these yogas help to purify the devotee's mind; however, the only purpose of practising them is to obtain the state of para bhakti. Para bhakti and jnana are one. When para bhakti manifests, one does not need to preach or practise vedanta; bhakti becomes vedanta. The real nature of God can only be reflected in a purified mind, and after the realization of this reflection, real love, para bhakti, for God is experienced.

In *Ramacharitamanas*, there is a story about Rama and Narada. Once, when Rama was gratified with Narada's devotion, he told him to ask for a boon. Narada replied, "O

Rama, if you must give me a boon, then grant that I may have pure love for you lotus feet and that I may not be deluded by your world-bewitching maya." Rama said, "I will grant you that, but ask for something more." Narada answered, "I do not want anything else. I want only pure love for your lotus feet, a love that seeks no return." This is called pure love; seeking God alone, and not asking Him for fame, bodily comforts, wealth or anything else.

For a devotee, God is real

In jnana yoga, the aspirant believes he is the supreme consciousness. In karma yoga, he feels that the whole world is a manifestation of God, and in raja yoga he thinks that the supreme consciousness is God. But the God of the highest bhakta is not an abstract, metaphysical or philosophical God. For him, God is as real as himself. He is a helper who is nearest to him, nearer than his own breath, his own mind or existence. Why should one depend on people like doctors, psychologists and teachers who have their own problems and frustrations? How can they help to relieve one's troubles and confusions? It is better to surrender to the One who can lead one to ultimate freedom, and to accept whatever He gives as His love. For a devotee, God can come in the form of a voice or person. He may come in any form because for him God exists in all forms.

Bhakti yoga says that one may love God as one loves one's husband or wife, child or father, friend or master. These are the different emotional attitudes through which one's love may be projected. Mirabai, a renowned Indian saint of the sixteenth century, was born a princess in a powerful west Indian state. When she was a little girl of eight or nine, a wandering mendicant presented her with a small idol of Krishna, the cowherd boy considered to be a perfect incarnation of the Supreme Being. Mira began worshipping the idol as her own husband. When the time came for her marriage, she said, "How can I marry another man when I am already married to my Lord Krishna?"

Her family and associates could not understand her innocent emotions, so she was married to a king who was very powerful, but not devoted. She was expected to behave like a queen, but was so intoxicated with love for Krishna that the palace could not contain her. Every evening she would go to the temple of her Lord and participate in devotional singing. Sometimes in sheer ecstasy she would dance with extreme joy and fall into blissful trances. The orthodox society of the time could not understand how the queen could behave in this way. Both her husband and mother-in-law became very angry and finally decided she should be killed.

In her poems Mira writes that she drank the cup of poison sent by the king and then laughed at it. The mother-in-law sent Mira a gift box filled with cobras. Opening the box, Mira found only an idol of Krishna. One night, when she was engrossed in her worship, hearing her voice, the king broke open her door, but found Mira alone inside. When he asked who she was speaking to, she replied, "To my beloved." "Who is your beloved? Where is he now?" asked the king. "Krishna is my beloved," she said. "I see Him, but how will you see Him when you don't love Him?"

> *Krishna is in my heart always.*
> *I have surrendered to my Lover*
> *And now I am His slave.*
> *I have won the grace of the Infinite Being*
> *And, friends, that's all that devotion means.*

Attaining divine love

In *Ramacharitamanas* (*Balkanda*: 144–151) the story of Manu and Satarupa is related. This ascetic royal couple performed great austerities in devotion to Sri Hari, depending solely upon the Lord for thousands of years. The omniscient Lord recognized them as His own servants, and when He manifested before them, He said, "Know that I am highly pleased with you. Ask of Me unreservedly for whatever boon you will."

On hearing Sri Hari's words, the king and queen said, "Now that we have seen Your lotus feet, all our desires have been fulfilled. Let us have attachment to Your feet of the same type as one has for a son. We pray that we could have a son like You. Let our lives be dependent on You; let us not survive without You."

The Lord granted the couple the boon they desired, saying, "Let it be so. After some time you will be born as the king and queen of Ayodhya; then I will be your son. I will perform sportive acts which will be a source of delight to My devotees. Hearing of My exploits with reverence, men will cross the ocean of worldly existence, renouncing the feeling of mineness and arrogance."

The best relationship one can have with God is one of love. To reach God, one only has to empty one's heart. One has to leave behind ego, caste, religion, children and wealth and stand before Him like a child. One has to discover how to relate to God. It is difficult, but once it is achieved, one will find the path.

Love has to be awakened if one wants to meet Him. People cherish love for mundane things, yet complain about failure in sadhana. They misappropriate their divine wealth to satisfy worldly whims and fancies, passions and fashions. Bhakti is a divine gift; it is given by Him, but it has been consumed by mundane objects. Ultimately, however, nobody knows how to develop divine love. It depends entirely on God's grace. Just as the chatak bird keeps its beak constantly open, waiting for the raindrops of *Swati nakshatra*, a constellation of heavenly bodies, so the devotee must keep his heart forever open. Maybe the drops of God's grace will one day descend on him.

When one lives only to experience the love of God, one must learn to detach from worldly existence by living in the world but not of it. In this way, all one's deepest samskaras can be removed, so that the love in one's heart flows out automatically and drowns all earthly desires as well as one's own self. Communion between the devotee and God takes place in this state of oneness, in the state of samarpan.

Glossary

Abhyasa – spiritual practice
Acharya – spiritual guide or teacher
Adharma – contrary to dharma or the natural order; disharmony; wrong actions
Adhimatra – element, material world
Adhimitra – intensity of earnestness
Adhyatmic – spiritual vibration
Adishakti – primal force behind creation
Advaita – non-dual; concept of oneness; monistic vision of reality
Advaita bhava – feeling of unity
Advaita jnana – realization of oneness, non-duality, unity
Advaita Vedanta – the philosophy of Vedanta which supports the view that the Supreme Being (Brahman) is the only eternal, unchanging reality; non-dualistic philosophy of Adi Shankaracharya
Agama – scriptures denoting the esoteric traditional worship of Devi tantric texts
Agastya – name of a celebrated saint
Agni – element of fire; god of fire and purification
Aham Brahmasmi – 'I am Brahman'; one of the four mahavakyas or greatest spiritual sayings of Advaita Vedanta
Ahamkara – ego; awareness of existence of 'I'
Ahimsa – absence of violence from within; non violence on every level to all living beings
Aishvarya – divine wealth of the Lord
Ajapa japa – continuous, spontaneous repetition of mantra
Ajna chakra – sixth pranic centre or chakra, situated at the top of the spinal cord; seat of intuition; psychic centre where guru's commands are received
Ajnana – ignorance; lack of wisdom
Akhara – traditionally a place for training in arms, particularly for sannyasins; place where sannyasins perform higher austerities in isolation
Amara – immortal
Ambarisha – a great devotee of Lord Rama
Amrita – nectar which bestows immortality
Anahata nada – unstruck sound reverberating throughout the universe; sound of the soul
Ananda – everlasting, pure bliss

Ananda swaroopa – essence of bliss
Anandamai Ma – Indian female saint
Anandamaya kosha – sheath or body of bliss
Anasakti – detachment
Anavasada – cheerfulness
Annamaya kosha – sheath or body of matter; food body
Antah karana – 'inner tool' of 'inner self'; internal organ of consciousness, comprising manas, chitta, buddhi and ahamkara
Antar atma – inner spirit or soul
Antaranga – internal
Anubhava roopa – state of divine oneness, one who is embraced by infinite love
Anuddharsha – absence of excessive hilarity
Anugraha – divine grace
Anushthana – resolve to perform mantra upasana for a particular period of time in one place, with absolute discipline
Apara bhakti – lower grade of bhakti: worshipping gods, visiting pilgrimage places, reading the scriptures, etc.
Apara vidya – empirical science, knowledge of the material, worldly aspects
Aparadha bhava – devotion with a sense of guilt
Aparigraha – not possessing objects beyond one's needs
Aparokshanubhuti – direct experience of God
Apta kama – perfected soul
Aradhana – fully immersed in worship of the deity with intense reverence
Archana – ritual worship of God with or without form or attributes
Ardhanarishwara – tantric symbol of the half-male-half-female form denoting the two principles of Shiva and Shakti
Arjuna – third Pandava, son of Indra and Kunti; in the *Bhagavad Gita* he received divine revelation from Lord Krishna
Arpan – the act of offering
Arta – devotee who worships God to alleviate personal distress and pain
Artha – wealth, material need, prosperity; accomplishment; attainment in all spheres of life; one of the four purusharthas
Artharthi – devotee who worships God to seek fulfilment of a personal desire
Asakti – attachment
Ashram – place of spiritual retreat and inner growth through internal and external labour
Atmabhava – attitude of perceiving and experiencing yourself in others
Atma jnana – direct knowledge of the Self
Atma krida – one who rejoices in the Self
Atma nivedana – absolute surrender of the Self; ninth stage of bhakti when the most subtle and final vestige of individual identity is dissolved in cosmic awareness

Atma rati – one who rejoices in the Self
Atma samarpan – absolute offering of the Self to the Divine
Atma – the Self beyond mind and body; superconsciousness, spirit, soul
Aum – or 'Om', universal mantra considered to be the origin of all other mantras; cosmic vibration of the universe
Avadhoota – one free from all worldly attachments or mental illusions, beyond duality; one who has transcended normal consciousness; sixth order of sannyasa tradition
Avatara – descent or advent of incarnations of God
Avidya – ignorance, illusion; lack of wisdom
Bhagavad Gita – 'Song of God'; Lord Krishna's teachings to Arjuna, delivered at the commencement of the battle of Kurukshetra during the great Mahabharata war
Bhagavata – realized saint
Bhajan – devotional song, hymn; adoration, worship
Bhakta – devotee of God
Bhakti – divine love; pure intense inner devotion or love; channelling of the intellect, emotions and Self towards a higher purpose
Bhakti marga – path of devotion or bhakti
Bharata – original name of India, literally, 'land engulfed in light'; the name of one of Lord Rama's brothers
Bhasma – sacred ash from the fire used in spiritual practices
Bhava – intense inner attitude or subtle emotion; state of being
Bhavana – feeling of devotion; ability to perceive subtle vibrations
Bhishma – great warrior of Mahabharata fame
Bhoga – craving for pleasure and enjoyment
Bija – seed; root mantra or syllable
Brahma – first of the Hindu trinity, God as Creator; divine spirit
Brahma bhava – highest state of realization
Brahma vidya – knowledge of God
Brahmacharya – living in constant awareness of Brahman; self-restraint; abstinence
Brahman – eternal, omnipresent principle of existence or ultimate reality
Brahmana – one seeking to know the Self
Brahmanistha – one established in direct knowledge of Brahman
Brahmavidya – knowledge of Brahman, the supreme existence
Buddha – illumined one; enlightened sage after whom Buddhism originated
Buddhi – higher intelligence concerned with real wisdom; intuitive aspect of consciousness by which the essential Self awakens to truth
Chaitanya Mahaprabhu – inspired sixteenth century bhakta from Bengal
Chakra – wheel or vortex; centre of energy or psychic centre
Chandala – an outcast, untouchable
Chetana – unmanifest aspect of consciousness

Chhandogya Upanishad – perhaps the oldest upanishad, part of the Sama Veda.
Chidakasha – space of the mind; the inner space seen whenever one closes one's eyes
Chitta – individual consciousness which includes the conscious, subconscious and unconscious dimensions of the mind; one of the four aspects of antah karana which receives impressions of experiences and stores them for future use in the form of samskaras
Chitta vritti – mental fluctuation, movement or modification
Daan – unconditional giving for the benefit of others
Dama – sense control
Darshan – inner vision of reality, God; to glimpse; to see an object without the medium of the senses, without thinking or feeling; to experience the fourth dimension of personality
Dasharatha – father of Lord Rama; an emperor of India who ruled as king of Ayodhya
Dasya bhava – cultivating the inner attitude of a servant to God
Dattatreya – sage of ancient India, considered to be an incarnation of Brahma, Vishnu and Shiva
Daya – mercy
Deity – form of divinity
Deva – illumined one; higher force or power; a self-luminous being in a male form
Devaki – earthly mother of Lord Krishna; wife of King Vasudeva
Devi Bhagavatam – scriptural text containing myths and doctrines of Devi
Devi – luminous being in a female aspect; divine force; manifestation of Shakti; goddess; Divine Mother
Dharana – concentration
Dharma – natural law; natural role one has to play in life; righteous action; duty, conduct; one of the four purushartha
Dhira – brave, steadfast
Dhyana – meditation; absorption in the object of worship or meditation
Dhyana yoga – spiritual path of self-introspection
Drashta – the inner witness or observer, the soul
Draupadi – great devotee and worshipper of Lord Krishna; daughter of King Drupada of Panchala; wife of the five Pandava brothers
Drishta – that which is seen
Dukha – grief
Dwesha – repulsion, dislike
Ekagrata – one-pointedness
Ekanath – a Maharastrian bhakta
Ganesha – elephant-headed, one tusked deity, son of Lord Shiva and Parvati; scribe of the Mahabharata; symbol of auspiciousness, wealth, knowledge, attainment and remover of obstacles

Gauranga – a Vaishnava saint
Gopis – cowherd girls, milkmaids in Vrindavan, who were the transcendental devotees of Lord Krishna
Gorakhnath – great yogi of the hatha yoga sect
Guna – quality inherent in nature, three in number: tamas, rajas and sattwa
Guru – dispeller of darkness; spiritually enlightened soul, who by the grace of his own atma can dispel darkness, ignorance and illusion from the mind of a disciple
Guru Granth Sahib – holy book of the Sikhs
Guru kripa – guru's grace
Guru Nanak – an enlightened sage who formed the Sikh religion
Guru Poornima – full moon day in July when all gurus are worshipped
Guru tattwa – inner essence, inherent element of guru in an individual
Hanuman – great devotee of Lord Rama; aided Rama in the rescue of Sita; considered to be the embodiment of devotion, strength and heroism; son of Pavan, god of the wind, and Anjana, a female monkey
Hari – a name of Vishnu
Hatha yoga – system of yoga consisting of practices for physical and mental purification
Havan – fire used in ceremonial worship
Himalayas – the great chain of rugged snow capped mountains running through north India, Pakistan, Nepal and Tibet; abode of the gods
Indra – god of the senses
Indriya – properties of the senses, sensory organs, ten in number; see *jnanendriyas* and *karmendriyas*
Ishta – chosen ideal; particular form of God one is devoted to
Ishta devata – one's personal deity, or favourite god
Ishta mantra – mantra of the chosen deity
Ishwara – higher reality; unmanifest existence
Ishwara pranidhana – cultivation of faith in the supreme or indestructible reality; surrender to God
Japa – repetition of a mantra or a name of God
Jignasu – spiritual seeker
Jiva – individual soul which passes through 8,400,000 births to obtain the human form
Jivanmukta – a soul who is liberated while living in the body
Jivatma – individual soul
Jnana – true knowledge; wisdom
Jnana yoga – path of intellectual enquiry into the nature of God
Jnanendriyas – organs of sense perception and knowledge: eyes, ears, nose, tongue and skin
Jnani – devotee who worships solely for divine knowledge, experience; wise person

Kaala – time in the absolute sense, or eternity; time principle; one of the five kanchukas or limiting aspects of energy which creates the dimension of time and restricts the individual within it

Kabir – religious reformer and saint; a great protagonist of Hindu-Muslim amity, influenced by Sufism

Kailash – Himalayan mountain; spiritual abode of Lord Shiva

Kaivalya – liberation from the cycle of births and deaths

Kala – creation, manifestation; one of the five kanchukas which restricts the creative power of individual consciousness

Kali – aspect of maha shakti, the destroyer of time and annihilator of the ego

Kali yuga – age of Kali; fourth and present age of the world, full of strife and evil

Kalpataru – wish fulfilling tree

Kalyana – auspicious; prosperity

Kama – need for emotional fulfilment; one of the four purushartha

Kamandalu – water pot traditionally carried by a sadhu

Kanchuka – invisible cloak of maya covering the individual self, which limits and restricts consciousness and creates the notion of duality; five in number: kala, avidyavidya, raga, niyati and kaala

Kanta bhava – devotion to the Lord like that of a devoted wife

Kapila – sage who founded Samkhya philosophy

Karma – action in the manifest and unmanifest dimension; law of cause and effect of three kinds: prarabdha, sanchit, kriyaman; action and result; also implies devoted action to alleviate the suffering of the afflicted

Karma yoga – perfected action; yoga of action; action performed with meditative awareness; yoga of dynamic meditation; yogic path of selfless service

Karmendriyas – five organs of action: hands, feet, vocal cords, tongue, excretory and reproductive organs

Karta – the doer

Kartritwa – doership

Karuna – compassion

Katha Upanishad – one of the principal upanishads in which Nachiketa speaks with Yama, the god of death

Kaushalya – wife of King Dasharatha, earthly mother of Lord Rama

Kirtan – singing God's name

Klesha – pain, anguish, affliction, distress, suffering

Koran – holy book of Islamic religion

Krishna – beloved of the gopis of Vrindavan; avatar, manifestation of God in human form who lived in Dwarpa yuga, eighth incarnation of Lord Vishnu, the cosmic sustainer; his teachings are recorded in the *Bhagavad Gita*

Kriya – action; motion; action leading to perfection of knowledge
Kriya yoga – practices of kundalini yoga
Kshama – patient, merciful
Kumkum – red powder used in rituals
Kundalini – divine energy that transforms human consciousness; evolutionary force; vital force or latent energy residing in mooladhara chakra, often referred to as the serpent power
Kundalini yoga – path of yoga which awakens the dormant spiritual force
Kunti – Lord Krishna's aunt, who invoked the Sun god through the power of mantra, thus creating her son Karna, who she abandoned to that god, in preference to her marriage with King Pandu
Laya – dissolution, merging
Lila – divine play, pastime; cosmic game of consciousness and energy; activity of prakriti and its three gunas
Madhurya bhava – most intense and sweetest love between lover and beloved, husband and wife
Maha – great
Maha bhava – great feeling or attitude of love
Mahayajna – great sacrificial rite
Mahatma – great soul
Mahavakyas – four great statements of the upanishads: 1. Prajnanam Brahma: Consciousness is Brahman; 2. Aham Brahmasmi: I am Brahman; 3. Tat Tvam Asi: You are That; 4. Ayam Atma Brahma: the Soul is Brahman
Mahima – greatness of the Lord
Maitreya – love; friendliness
Mamata – feeling of attachment
Manas – analytical, lower or empirical mind; aspect of manifest mind involved in experiences of sensory perception and thought/counter-thought
Mantra – subtle sound or combinations of sound vibrations revealed to sages in deep meditation, used for liberating consciousness from the limitations of mundane awareness
Marga – path
Maya – illusion; cause of the phenomenal world
Milarepa – enlightened Tibetan yogi
Mirabai – female saint of the early sixteenth century; great devotee of Lord Krishna
Moha – confusion, delusion
Moksha – liberation, freedom from the cycles of birth, death and rebirth
Moksha sadhaka – one who lives life only to attain liberation
Mouna – restrained speech; silence
Mukti – salvation, emancipation, liberation, freedom
Mumukshutva – intense desire for liberation

Mumukshu – seeker of liberation
Murti – idol of worship
Naam sankirtan – group chanting of God's name
Naam smarana – remembrance of God's name
Nachiketa – name of the seeker and principal character in the Katha Upanishad
Nada – psychic or eternal sound vibrations heard in the meditative state
Naham bhokta – 'I am not the enjoyer'
Naham karta – 'I am not the doer'
Narada, Devarishi – divine personality, sage, lawgiver or political philosopher mentioned in the *Rigveda*, *Ramayana* and *Mahabharata*
Narayana – epithet of Vishnu, the supporter of life
Navadha bhakti – nine stages of bhakti
Neti-neti – doctrine of 'Not this, not this'; a famous exclamation of the upanishads related to the impossibility of reducing divinity to any explanation or definition
Nimitta bhava – the attitude of being an instrument in the hands of God
Nirakara – formless, without form; unmanifest; the culmination of sakara (with form)
Nirguna – a form free of all gunas; without qualities
Nirodha – state of mind beyond the three gunas; complete cessation of patterns of consciousness when the mind is under perfect control
Nirvana – higher state of existence; cessation of suffering; final liberation
Nirvikalpa – without any modification or thought
Nirvikalpa samadhi – state in which the mind ceases to function and only pure consciousness remains
Nishkama – selfless, desireless; actions performed without any expectation of reward
Nishtha – devoutness, steadfastness
Nityananda – eternal, uninterrupted bliss
Nityatwa roopa – form of consciousness denoting the eternal attribute of creation
Nivritti – path in which one pursues a desire to obtain freedom and liberation; path of non-indulgence
Niyama – five personal purificatory observances which render the mind tranquil for meditation: shaucha or cleanliness, santosha or contentment, tapas or austerity, swadhyaya or self-study, ishwara pranidhana or surrender to God, as defined in the second stage of Patanjali's ashtanga yoga
Niyati – destiny
Nyasa – trust
Om – or 'Aum', universal mantra; the origin of all other mantras; cosmic vibration of the universe
Om Namah Shivaya – Shiva mantra; 'I salute Shiva'

Om Tat Sat – 'God is Truth'
Pada – path, way
Paramahamsa – 'supreme swan'; high order of sannyasins who are able to discriminate between reality and unreality; having completed their work, paramahamsa sannyasins devote themselves totally to sadhana, thus approaching the final goal of moksha or self liberation
Paramartha – highest truth
Para bhakta – supreme devotee; one who constantly worships God as the one essence in all forms
Para bhakti – supreme or transcendental bhakti
Para vairagya – absence of attachment in any form; highest type of vairagya, dispassion
Para vidya – higher knowledge, transcendental knowledge, direct knowledge of Brahman
Patanjali – rishi who codified the stages of meditation in the system of raja yoga; author of *Yoga Sutras*
Path – recitation of a sacred text
Pooja – worship, usually accompanied by precise ritual to bring devotee into the proximity of God
Pooja bhava – attitude of worshipping God through one's actions in daily life; external worship
Poorna – completeness, wholeness
Poornatwa – element of wholeness, the completeness of creation
Prahlada – great bhakta of Lord Vishnu
Prakriti – manifest and unmanifest nature composed of the three gunas or attributes; active principle of the manifest world; vehicle of purusha or consciousness
Prana – vital energy
Pranam – reverential salutation, obeisance, prostration
Pranayama – yogic technique which expands the dimensions of vital or pranic energy (life force) through breath control
Prarabdha karma – destined action; unalterable or fixed karma; the portion of karma that determines one's present life and cannot be averted
Prarthana – worship through prayer
Prasad – blessed gift or object; grace; happiness, delight and joy
Pratyahara – withdrawing the senses from external objects; prerequisite for dharana and higher stages of meditation; fifth limb of Patanjali's ashtanga yoga
Pravritti – path of involvement in the world
Prema bhava – highest feeling or love for God
Prema bhakta – devotee who loves God only for love's sake
Puranas – ancient texts concerning the earliest mythology of the tantric and vedic traditions

Purascharana – form of mantra upasana, involving repetition of a mantra hundreds of thousands of times within a specified period of time, while following definite rules for the practice

Purusha – soul; totality of consciousness; pure consciousness

Purushartha – personal effort; four areas of human endeavour to be fulfilled: artha or wealth, kama or love, dharma or duty, and moksha or liberation

Purushottama – highest purusha, supreme spirit

Radha – foremost transcendental lover and devotee of Lord Krishna; chief of the gopis, milkmaids

Raga – attachment, association, identification, whether external or internal

Raja yoga – eightfold path classified by Patanjali in the *Yoga Sutras*; system of yoga which awakens the psychic awareness and faculties through meditation, culminating in samadhi

Rajas – one of the three gunas, representing the dynamic, active state of mind and nature

Rama – hero of the *Ramayana*; seventh incarnation of Vishnu, embodiment of dharma

Ramacharitamanas – life story of Lord Rama as a devotional, poetic composition written by Tulsidas, in Avadhi, a local dialect

Ramakrishna Paramahamsa – renowned mystic and prema bhakta from Bengal

Ramana Maharshi – realized saint and jnana yogi from south India, who taught awareness of pure consciousness through self-enquiry

Ramanuja – founder of the Vishishta Advaita school of philosophy

Ramayana – an inspired book in verses describing the life of the avatara Lord Rama; the historical version is written by Valmiki in Sanskrit, and the devotion version authored by Tulsidas

Rasa – blissful essence of love

Rati – intense love or attachment to God that softens the heart

Rishi – seer of truth; realized sage

Rishi Vishwamitra – name of a celebrated sage

Roopa – form

Roopa shakti – love of His enchanting beauty and form

Sadhaka – spiritual aspirant established in sadhana

Sadhana – spiritual practice performed regularly for attainment of inner experience and self-realization

Sadhu – spiritual mendicant; one who regularly performs spiritual practices for enlightenment over a long period of time, with faith and devotion

Sahaja -- spontaneous, easy, natural

Sahasrara – abode of superconsciousness; highest psychic centre which symbolizes the threshold between the psychic and spiritual realms, located at the crown of the head

Sakara – with form

Sakhya bhava – cultivating the attitude of a friend with God
Sakshi bhava – attitude of remaining the witness
Sama – tranquil, equipoised
Sama drishti – equal vision
Sama Veda – Veda primarily of devotion, worship and contemplation; third of the four Vedas
Samadhana – mental equilibrium
Samadhi – culmination of meditation; final stage of raja yoga
Samarpan – total offering of one's entire self to God; relinquish, surrender
Samarpan muhurta – moment of dedication
Samsara – illusory world, cycle of birth, death and rebirth, transmigration
Sanat Kumara – guru of Devarishi Narada, a prince among bhaktas
Sanatana dharma – system of eternal values underlying the vedic civilization
Sandilya – author of *Sandilya Sutra*; great acharya in the path of bhakti
Sankalpa – positive resolve; will, determination, conviction
Sankirtan – collective chanting of God's name with musical instruments
Sannyasa – dedication; complete renunciation of the world, its possessions and attachments
Sannyasin – renunciate; one who has taken sannyasa initiation; one who is not dependent on the results of action; trustee
Sanyam – action with discrimination and non-attachment; self-restraint
Sarva – whole, entire, total, all
Sarva kartritwa roopa – power to create the entire universe from nothing
Sarva tattwa roopa – all the elements necessary for creation
Sarva tyaga – renunciation of everything
Satguru – subtle, inner essence of guru
Satsang – gathering of spiritually minded people in which the ideals and principles of truth are discussed; association, being in the company of saints or the wise
Sattwa – one of the three gunas; pure, unadulterated quality; state of luminosity and harmony
Satyam – truth, reality
Seva – service; offering oneself wholly to the service of God, guru or the spiritual preceptor; selfless external and internal activity, social and spiritual, to channel the senses, mind and ego
Shabari – a tribal who had intense love for Lord Rama
Shadsampat – sixfold virtues: tranquillity, restraint, renunciation, endurance, faith and balance of mind
Shakta – worshipper of Devi
Shakti – primal energy; manifest consciousness; subtle creative and vital energy; counterpart of Shiva
Shankaracharya – enlightened sage who revitalized the Shaivite tradition, expounded and spread the Adwaita Vedanta philosophy throughout India, and founded the Dashnami order of sannyasa

Shastra – scripture; sacred book
Shishya – disciple
Shiva – 'auspicious one'; symbol of supreme consciousness; male principle; cosmic consciousness; first yogi; last of the Hindu trinity, representing the destructive or transformative aspect of ego
Shoonya – void, vacuum, nothingness
Shraddha – faith, trust; belief in divine revelation
Siddha – perfected being; sage, seer
Siddhi – psychic ability; control of mind and power; supernatural powers obtained by yogis as a result of sustained practice
Sirshasana – head stand pose
Sita – incarnation of Shakti as the wife of Lord Rama
Sloka – scriptural verse
Smarana – constant remembrance of God's name
Smriti – memory; vedic texts transmitted by memory
Sneha – affection, love, kindness
Srimad Bhagavatam – sacred book, vedic text recounting the life of Lord Krishna and his devotees
Surdas – blind Indian poet saint of the bhakti movement, composer of devotional songs and great bhakta of Lord Rama
Surya – vital pranic energy; sun; the sun god; symbol of the atma
Sushupti – deep sleep or unconsciousness realm of mind
Swabhava – inherent nature
Swadhyaya – self-study and study of devotional books
Swapna – subconscious real of mind, state of dreaming
Swati nakshatra – a particular constellation of heavenly bodies
Tamas – one of the three gunas; quality of inertia, dullness or ignorance
Tanmaya shakti – love of complete absorption in Him
Tantra – ancient universal science, philosophy and culture which deals with the transcendence of human nature from the present mundane level of evolution and understanding to the highest attainment of transcendental awareness, knowledge and experience; process of expansion of mind and liberation of energy; one of the six classical Indian philosophies
Tapasya – practice of austerity; process of burning impurities
Tattwa – essential element, essence; true or real state
Tirtha – place of pilgrimage
Titiksha – power of endurance; bearing all afflictions; one of the sixfold virtues of sadhana
Tulsidas – famous Indian saint who wrote *Ramacharitamanas*, the story of Lord Rama
Turiya – the witnessing or transcendental consciousness which links waking, dreaming and deep sleep states

Tyaga – renunciation or gradual dissociation of the mind from worldly objects and the seed of desire
Tyagi – one who has renounced
Uddhava – devotee of Lord Krishna
Unmani – 'no mind'; centre beyond mind and thought where the mind is turned completely inwards
Upadesha – spiritual instruction, guidance
Upadhi – limiting adjunct; any superimposition that gives a limited view of the Absolute
Upanishads – 'to sit close by and listen'; ancient vedic texts, conveyed by sages, rishis or seers containing their experiences and teachings on the ultimate reality
Uparati – abstaining from worldly enjoyments; one of the sixfold virtues
Upasana – in the proximity of God; sitting near the Lord; personalized form of worship
Vaikuntha – spiritual abode of Lord Krishna
Vairagya – non-attachment, dispassion, detachment from the world and its cause
Valmiki – rishi who wrote the *Ramayana*
Vandana – prostration, prayer to God; sixth of the nine modes of upasana, worship
Varuna – god of water
Vasana – seed or inherent desire; subtle desire of the unconsciousness
Vasishtha – celebrated seer, family priest of the solar race of kings and author of *Yoga Vasishtha* and several vedic hymns; guru of Lord Rama and his family
Vasudeva – a name of Krishna
Vatsalya bhava – attitude of love of a parent to a child
Vedanta – 'end of perceivable knowledge'; one of the six darshanas or systems of the vedic philosophy which deals with transcendental and manifest nature of consciousness
Vedas – most ancient scriptural texts of Sanatana dharma, composed before 5,000 BC, revealed to the sages and expressing knowledge of the whole universe; the four Vedas are: Rig, Yajur, Sama and Atharva
Veera bhava – feeling one has towards an enemy
Vibhishana – a great devotee of Lord Rama
Vidya – inner knowledge, spiritual knowledge
Vijnanamaya kosha – higher mental sheath or body
Vimoha – freedom from desires
Vishnu – the aspect of the Supreme concerned with maintenance or preservation; sustainer of the universe
Vishnu Sahasranama – one thousand names in praise of Lord Vishnu, the preserver of the universe
Viveka – discrimination; right knowledge or understanding

Vrata – resolution to carry out a vow under strict rules
Vrindavan – place where Lord Krishna performed his lila
Vritti – circle, pattern of the mind; mental modification
Vyapatattwa – all-pervading, omnipresent attribute of consciousness
Vyasa – author of *Mahabharata*, *Brahma Sutra*, and codifier of the Vedas
Yajna – worship through sacrifice or sacrificial rite for internal and external purification; offering oblations to the fire; any work beneficial for one and all
Yama – self restraints or rules of conduct which render the emotions tranquil: ahimsa or non-violence, satya or truth, asteya or non-stealing, brahmacharya or continence, aparigraha or non-covetousness
Yoga – union; from *yuj* to yoke; system of thought and practices leading to a state of union between two opposite poles, i.e. individual and universal awareness; one of the six classical Indian philosophies
Yoga shastras – yoga system of philosophy and practice aiming to teach union of the human soul with the supreme spirit
Yoga Sutras – ancient authoritative text on raja yoga by Rishi Patanjali
Yoga Vasishtha – a most ancient and famous scripture on Vedanta in the form of a dialogue between Lord Rama and his guru, Vasishtha